C000060702

DIAMOND
GEEZERS

KRIS HOLLINGTON

DIAMOND GEEZERS

The Inside Story of the Crime of the Millennium

Michael O'Mara Books Limited

First published in Great Britain in 2004 by
Michael O'Mara Books Ltd
9 Lion Yard, Tremadoc Road
London SW4 7NQ

Copyright © 2004 Kris Hollington

The right of Kris Hollington to be identified as the author of this work
has been asserted by him in accordance with the Copyright, Designs and
Patents Act 1988.

All rights reserved. No part of this publication may be reproduced, stored
in a retrieval system, or transmitted by any means, without the prior permission
in writing of the publisher, nor be otherwise circulated in any form of binding or
cover other than that in which it is published and without a similar condition
including this condition being imposed on the subsequent purchaser.

Every effort has been made to trace and contact copyright holders of all
materials in this book. The author and publishers will be glad to rectify any
omissions at the earliest opportunity.

A CIP catalogue record for this book is available from the British Library.

ISBN 1-84317-122-8

1 3 5 7 9 10 8 6 4 2

www.mombooks.com

Designed and typeset by www.envydesign.co.uk

Colour plates section designed by Button Group plc

Printed and bound in England by Clays Ltd, St Ives plc

CONTENTS

PICTURE ACKNOWLEDGEMENTS

All plate-section photographs and the cover photograph of the Millennium Star are courtesy of the Metropolitan Police Clips, with the following exceptions:

Front cover:

Main photograph: Tony Stone

Security camera: istockphoto.com

Plate section:

Page 1, bottom: Christina Lister/REX FEATURES

Page 3, top, and 5, bottom: Nick Razzell/REX FEATURES

Page 4, top: TopFoto/English Heritage/HIP

Page 5, above left: REX FEATURES

Page 5, above right: Kent News & Pictures/CORBIS SYGMA

Page 8, top: Andrew Murray/REX FEATURES

1 – HIGHWAY ROBBERY

'Where's the bloody river?'

UNKNOWN ARMED ROBBER MAKING HIS GETAWAY

7.45 a.m., 7 July 2000, Aylesford, Kent. The nine men watched hungrily as their target travelled towards them carrying its £8.7 million cash payload. Two of the robbers, sitting in the back of a dark blue Ford Transit van, gripped their sawn-off shotguns tightly, their white knuckles hidden by tight black leather gloves. Two more lowered their balaclavas and picked up large circular saws from the van floor. As the Securicor van passed them on its journey to a depot in Aylesford in leafy Kent, the wheelman pulled out into the traffic and followed.

The gang were about to make one of the most daring robbery attempts in British criminal history. If successful, it would net them almost £1 million pounds apiece. If they failed, they were looking at ten years-to-life in prison. But for these hardened pros, failure was not an option. The job had been touted around a close-knit group of professional robbers based in South London for several weeks. Eventually, the gang complete, they met each other on a Kent farm the night before the raid. It was like an odd reunion of sorts, mercenaries of a variety of shapes, sizes and ages pulled together by a common desire for lots of hard cash. The men were too keyed up to sleep much and stayed up most of the night, crowded around the kitchen table and in the farmhouse's lounge, buzzing at the thought of the drama that would unfold tomorrow. Conversation inevitably centred on the work they loved. There were no nerves, only excitement and a determination to get the job done. Their resolve had been reinforced as they climbed into the van in the early-morning light, and now, as the driver flicked the indicator and moved across to the outside lane of the quiet through road, the engine's rising tone was matched by the robbers' rising adrenalin as the accelerator was pressed close to the floor. Before the security guards could react to the shock of seeing a balaclava-clad driver overtaking them, the robbers' van had swerved in front and gradually slowed, forcing the security van driver to a stop. As soon as it had come to a halt, the youngest, thinnest and most reckless of the gang, who had been lying in wait by the roadside, dived underneath the van and cut the brake lines before the driver could find reverse gear. The security guards, realizing they were the victims of a hold-up, called for help on the radio while the driver frantically but futilely grappled with the gears. But because the brakes had been cut, the van failed to move. The route behind them was now blocked by the gang's second vehicle and secret weapon, an articulated lorry, which had reversed from a side street into position and was revving its engine menacingly.

The robbers poured out of the Transit. Almost instantly, one of the team fired two shots into the air, letting the security guards know they meant business. The driver of the security van noticed that the man who fired the shotgun was wearing glasses. A 6-foot 4-inch overweight giant ran to the front of the security van and looked in the driver's window. The terrified guards watched helplessly as the giant smiled and waved at them a pair of ominous-looking green discs topped with red flashing lights. He then clamped the discs on the van's bonnet and mouthed the word 'Boom!' while showing them a remote-control device. The security guards knew then that to try anything heroic was pointless and could do nothing else but pray that they would live through the experience.

The two men carrying the petrol-driven cutting machines sprinted to the back of the security van and attempted to saw away the tailgate, which acts as an extra layer of protection for the rear doors. After a short shower of yellow sparks, they shouted that the cutters were not making any headway — but they had half-expected them to fail. 'Gertie' was then brought into play. Gertie was the 7-ton lorry waiting behind the security van. The suspension had been removed to increase its effectiveness as a ramming vehicle. Fitted to the back of the ten-wheeler was a sharp, greased and concrete-filled metal spike. Gertie was lined up facing away from the van, with the point of the spike about 50 yards away. The gears were ground into reverse and then the wheelman floored the accelerator. The plan was that Gertie would make a hole in the van doors large enough to throw in an improvised anchor. Gertie would then accelerate away, ripping the doors off and exposing the full-to-bursting money sacks.

The fat robber standing at the front of the van waved to the petrified security guards, blew them a kiss goodbye and stood back a few paces. The guards thought their number had come up as they heard Gertie screaming towards them. The lorry crashed into the rear doors, throwing the two men around the cab like rag dolls. The spike tore the metal and pierced the doors, making a small hole, but it wasn't enough. Gertie's wheelman prepared her for another run-up.

The roads were getting congested, as the ongoing robbery was blocking a busy through road. The robbers had expected this. For them it was good news, as it meant the police would be hampered reaching the scene. The northbound side of a nearby dual carriageway was also becoming congested with rubbernecks. The gang were running out of time. Confused and angry early-motoring commuters, who were doing their best to try to dodge the mayhem, were fast realizing what was happening and had begun dialling 999 on their mobiles. At 7.55 a.m., the normally quiet switchboard at Kent police headquarters was suddenly jammed with dozens of calls. A nearby traffic vehicle was immediately dispatched to the scene and backup called for.

Gertie crashed into her hapless victim yet again. By now the payload was visible, but it had taken too long. The driver of the lead police car was a master of his craft and was weaving through traffic with brilliant expertise, far faster than the robbers had believed possible. As the car shifted gear and bounced over a traffic island, the robbers heard the sirens. Each of them saw the determined progress of the police in their mind's eye and subsequently how much time they would have to spend in jail if caught. Their leader turned and looked back over his shoulder towards the approaching siren and reluctantly called it a day. As they fled down a side street, one of the gang was heard to shout: 'Where's the bloody river?'

They left pandemonium behind them on the motorway. The security guards had run from the vehicle yelling at the public to get out of their cars and move back and then informed the shocked traffic policemen that the vehicle was set to explode. Five minutes after the robbers had fled, the police had cordoned off the area and had put out a call to the bomb-disposal squad, who were immediately scrambled from their base at RAF Folkestone.

Meanwhile, a local man was walking his dog along the towpath of the River Medway when he heard the roar of an engine and was stunned to see a 25-foot day cruiser with its cover up recklessly sweep past at about 25 to 30 miles per hour, which was dangerously fast for this section of the river. The wash from the boat covered the towpath and nearly swept his dog away.

The would-be robbers had arrived at a prearranged meeting point on the bank of the River Medway. They set fire to the van, boarded a waiting speedboat and sped downstream. They had escaped, albeit empty-handed. As they bombed down the Medway past the early-morning dog-walker, one of the gang pulled off his balaclava. He looked far too old to be an armed robber. His name was Terence Millman. His face was covered in sweat and he was breathing hard but laughing. 'Oh well, never mind, lads,' he winked at the other men. 'Steak-and-kidney pie, anyone?'

Police officers had just got themselves behind the police line when a fully armoured member of the bomb-disposal team lifted one of the devices off the vehicle. He waddled towards the police cordon. Puzzled officers saw that he was smiling. He said, 'Cheeky bastards,' and waved the device under a shocked PC's nose. The constable watched as he turned it over. It was a Fray Bentos steak-and-kidney-pie tin painted green with a light on top and a battery and magnet fastened underneath.

2 – A STAR IS BORN

'The most beautiful diamond I have ever seen.'

HARRY OPPENHEIMER, FORMER CHAIRMAN OF DE BEERS

The Millennium Star, arguably the world's most beautiful diamond, was born deep in the dark heart of Africa – Mbuji-Mayi, to be precise, a tough mineral-trading town located within the jungle interior of the Democratic Republic of Congo, one of the most inaccessible places in the world.

Despite its remoteness, Mbuji-Mayi is a bustling metropolis with a population of around 500,000, of whom 30,000 are diamond prospectors. Surrounded by the lush Congo jungle and cut in two by the meandering brown Sankuru River, this overcrowded town is a hellish-looking blot on the landscape, writhing with poverty and disease. Cholera epidemics sweep through its haphazard, ramshackle streets with alarming regularity and devastation. Its isolation means that the law in Mbuji-Mayi is arbitrary, and the boiling temperatures only serve to add to the inter-tribal tensions, which have already claimed 3.3 million lives in civil wars since 1998.

The Democratic Republic of Congo is abundant in natural wealth: gold, diamonds, timber, oil, rubber and even the mobile-phone mineral coltan. Foreign companies, happy to cut deals with military commanders, have sustained conflicts by exploiting these natural resources with a general disregard for human rights or long-term development. The West has played a major role in the devastation of this region's resources and people.

The flood plains of Mbuji-Mayi are home to the world's most flawless diamonds and, as a result, every kind of prospector, from the multinational to the lone digger, heads to the area, each hoping to get lucky and find that unique diamond, or diamond seam, which will make their fortunes. Greed and desperation usually override the fear of death at the cruel hands of the militia, but in the spring of 1992 even the most hardened adventurers were leaving the dusty, baking settlement as what was then called the Republic of Zaire fell apart in one of the most bloody revolutionary periods in its history.

Those foolhardy enough continued to dig and, a few miles upstream from the town centre, two of the town's 'pickers', the poorest miners who scrape a meagre living digging shallow holes for tiny alluvial diamonds, scratched at the drought-ridden river beds with bent and rust-coated shovels. Suddenly, in the bright sunlight, something flashed at the two diggers, who stopped what they were doing and looked at each other, neither daring to voice his hopes.

They bent down and brushed some of the dust away. A chunk of what appeared to be glass became visible. They dug deeper into the dry, cracked soil until they eased out an enormous diamond, the size and shape of a spearhead. It was a birth millions of years in the making, and the end of a journey of several miles through the earth's crust. The gem glinted with impossible brightness in the white light of the afternoon sun.

The pickers turned it over and over, looking for a flaw, a crack in the diamond wrought by the millions of tons of rock it had passed through on its way to the earth's surface. There was none. In silent reverence for what they had found, they wrapped the jewel carefully in a shirt and quietly made their way to the offices of the only company in the Congo able to afford such a monster of a gem.

Gary Ralfe, De Beers' managing director, recalled how he was told of the discovery: 'These people were just scratching around, found the diamond and brought it to our office in Mbuji-Mayi,' he said. 'They arrived late at night, and I was rung just as I was going to bed.'

At first, Ralfe couldn't believe it and thought that the diamond was simply a piece of glass. When weighed, the uncut diamond was a staggering 777 carats.

With the help of a negotiator, the tribesmen eventually sold it to De Beers for £400,000, but at first the company would not confirm this. A spokesman did then state that the discovery had since made them millionaires, although it was not clear what use money was to two bushmen without a bank account. De Beers had to open one for them.

Following the discovery, a 'diamond rush' threatened to swamp Mbuji-Mayi. The steel doors of De Beers' Mbuji-Mayi office, however, remained firmly closed to traders until the massive diamond could be shipped out twenty-four hours later under armed guard. As for the two pickers, they promptly disappeared and were never heard of again. Rumours have since spread that on the very next day they were captured, tortured and killed by the local militia for not paying them a cut.

De Beers, recognizing the uniqueness of the gem, decided that it would be held back and its existence kept secret until 1999, when it would be used to commemorate the millennium. It was duly named the Millennium Star and became the centrepiece of the Millennium Collection, which would also contain the most flawless blue diamonds mined from De Beers' premier mine in South Africa.

The cutting of the Millennium Star set international precedents in the diamond industry. Five of the world's leading diamond cutters spent six months agonizing over a variety of designs and possibilities before a single cut was authorized. In order to cut and polish the stone, a special 'operating theatre' was built, not dissimilar to the conditions in a sterile hospital room. No dust was allowed to touch the stone, and the temperature was carefully controlled to avoid cracks developing. The South African, Israeli, Belgian and American workers painstakingly transformed the flawless, elongated rough stone into a classic pear-shaped gem over the course of three years.

They decided to cut the rough stone into three pieces, of which the Millennium Star is the largest. The cutters were tight-lipped about what happened to the other two but these 'offcuts', also known as 'granny diamonds', were in fact cut in a variety of shapes and, although stunning, are dwarfed by the 2-inch-long Millennium Star.

When completed, it was evident to all that the Millennium Star was the finest diamond De Beers had ever owned since the company was founded in 1888. The ninety-one-year-old former chairman and doyen of the industry, Harry Oppenheimer, described it as 'the most beautiful diamond I have ever seen'. It is the world's largest colourless, internally and externally flawless pear-shaped diamond. De Beers refuse point-blank to put a price on it. Estimates made by the media hovered around the £100 million mark. Up until then, the previous record price paid for any polished diamond was $16 million (£9 million) for the flawless 100.1-carat the Star of the Season at a Sotheby's auction in May 1999.

In addition to the Millennium Star, the Millennium Collection also consisted of eleven highly unusual blue diamonds cut into a variety of shapes, with a total weight of 118 carats. They ranged in size from 5.16 carats to a phenomenal 27.64-carat heart-shaped stone, the Heart of Eternity. The blue diamonds, although not as remarkable as the Millennium Star, were none the less among the finest jewels in the world. Only one significant blue diamond is mined per year, and De Beers will pay out a large bonus to the lucky finder. The best blue diamonds are greatly admired and eagerly sought after by collectors and connoisseurs. Of the ten highest per-carat prices paid for coloured diamonds at auction, six have been blue diamonds. One 20-carat blue stone fetched over $10 million (£5.5 million).

After nearly six years of searching for the perfect blue stones, the De Beers Millennium Collection was complete. It was presented to the world with great theatre during an impressive ceremony on the top floor of De Beers' Fort Knox-like offices in Charterhouse Street, which overlooks London's famous Hatton Garden diamond market, in September 1999. Usually, De Beers are loath to draw any attention to their London headquarters, and no sign identifies the building. But this was a very special occasion, and, besides, their security measures are the most advanced on the planet. Secret cameras hidden in walls cover every inch of space and are powerful enough to capture the colour of a person's eyes.

In an elaborate display, the eleven diamonds orbited the Millennium Star like sparkling blue satellites. The Star was then carefully lifted and lovingly caressed by the latest Bond girl, French actress Sophie Marceau, who starred with Pierce Brosnan in *The World Is Not Enough*, while the collection was introduced by the De Beers chairman, Nicky Oppenheimer. The flamboyant grandson of De Beers' founder, sometimes called 'the Cuban' because he sports a Fidel Castro-style beard, took over as chairman in 1998. Anyone who saw him on the day the Millennium Collection was unveiled could not help but admire his enthusiasm and rhetoric. Oppenheimer, waving his arms and perspiring with the excitement of finally sharing the Millennium Collection with the rest of the world after six years of secrecy, gave an emotional speech at the glamorous reception: 'As we come together to celebrate the new millennium, De Beers is giving the world a chance to see this unique collection – truly a once-in-a-millennium experience. To be able, therefore, to unveil a truly spectacular new diamond on the threshold of the new millennium is surely a uniquely apposite combination of two very rare events. To be able to unveil not only one diamond but a collection of such rarity that most of us will not see its like again is, I think, the only adequate way to mark the passage of 2,000 years of man's history.'

Of course, the Millennium Collection existed for another reason apart from the commemoration of 2,000 years of human history. In North America and Europe alone, De Beers predicted that there would be 7 million engagements, 28 million weddings, 69 million births and 880 million anniversaries celebrated in 2000. If just 1 in 360 among this group bought a diamond to commemorate the occasion, world diamond sales would jump 10 per cent, meaning an extra $1 billion in De Beers' coffers.

De Beers wanted the public to go diamond crazy for the millennium.

To generate interest, the company needed publicity, and that publicity came in the form of those most exquisite, perfectly formed diamonds in the world, the Millennium Collection.

De Beers also decided to release 20,000 of the highest-quality 1- and 2-carat diamonds held in its massive diamond stockpile. These were called the De Beers Millennium Diamonds, and each was inscribed with a number, the name of one of the brightest stars in the heavens and the De Beers centenary logo. The inscription required 200-times magnification to be made readable. The packaging included an individual hologrammed identity card with an enlargement of the stone's unique inscription, such as Altair 101. This high-tech element was designed with the idea of catching the imagination of the mostly male buyers of diamonds. The limited edition commanded a substantial premium (each diamond costing somewhere around £10,000). De Beers hoped that it would instil enthusiasm for other diamond purchases during 2000.

But like most global conglomerates, De Beers wanted to do something extra special for the new millennium, something that would put them on the world stage for 2000, something that would keep diamonds in the public eye. Luckily, a perfect opportunity presented itself. The organizers of London's Millennium Dome approached De Beers, fearing that the site of the millennium celebrations in the UK 'lacked glamour'. There was a feeling among the organizers that while there were plenty of exhibits inside the Dome, there were not enough genuine 'marvels' and 'wonders of the world' to be seen that would draw in the crowds. The New Millennium Experience Company hoped that the Collection would attract as much public interest as the Koh-i-Noor diamond ('Mountain of Light') did when it was displayed at the Great Exhibition at Crystal Palace in 1851. However, the Koh-i-Noor already had a dramatic 500-year history, while the Star, a young diamond, was yet to gain notoriety. De Beers decided to take a gamble: this was their chance to thrust themselves into the centre of the UK's millennium celebrations and gain precious worldwide publicity. In October 1999 the Oppenheimers visited the site and, much to the NMEC's delight, they liked what they saw. It was eventually agreed that De Beers would provide £2 million in sponsorship for the Dome, most of which would be spent on security for the Collection. In return, De Beers got the perfect advertising for the new millennium.

The Dome was and still is the most controversial building in Britain. It was to be the focus of the millennium celebrations in the UK and was also meant to be a portrait of the nation. Minister for the Dome, Peter Mandelson, described its *raison d'être* in 1999: 'The millennium project is an opportunity for people to take stock, to pause and to reflect on the nature of our society in all its dimensions, spiritual as well as any other, and to consider what sort of country and society we want to live in as we enter the new century and the new millennium. In that sense the project will be inspiring and challenging, as well as enormous fun.' Peter Mandelson is the grandson of Herbert Morrison, who organized the 1951 Festival of Britain, which lifted Britain out of the post-war doldrums. It also had a dome, with 'zones' (Land, Sea, Space, Sky, Earth, the Living World, etc.) and was a resounding success.

The Millennium Dome was only a temporary project, however, and would be open to anyone prepared to stump up the £20 entrance fee for one year and then ... well, its future was as uncertain then as it is now. Sitting on the South Bank of the River Thames, a stone's throw from the prime meridian in Greenwich, the Dome looks like a downed flying saucer from a 1950s B-movie and has been compared with everything from Xanadu to a giant contraceptive device. But the Millennium Dome's sheer scale and design are breathtaking. The structure is massive, with an overall circumference of over half a mile and a height of 165 feet at its central point. It encloses a ground-floor area of over 80,000 square feet. It can contain 12 football pitches, 1,100 Olympic-sized swimming pools or 18,000 double-decker London buses. It would take Niagara Falls about fifteen minutes to fill the Dome. In 2000 the interior of the Dome consisted of a 12,000-seat arena encircled by 14 different zones (Money, Mind, Body, Planet and so on), each containing themed exhibits.

Since the Dome's inception under John Major's Conservative

government, many critics predicted its doom. The overwhelming barrage of criticism forced the Labour government, which took control of the project in 1997, to over-promote what has now become a billion-pound behemoth. Peter Mandelson remarked in February 1998: 'If it is a success, it will never be forgotten. If it's a failure, we shall never be forgiven.' When asked for a comment on the Dome in September 2000, his spokesman said: 'I will ask him, but don't hold your breath.'

Deputy Prime Minister John Prescott, who helped to persuade Tony Blair to back the project, said in June 1997: 'If we can't make this work, we're not much of a government.' Tony Blair famously said in 1999 that the Dome is to be 'the first paragraph of my next election manifesto'. In the programme for the opening ceremony, Mr Blair wrote: 'This truly remarkable structure and the Millennium Experience inside it have achieved worldwide recognition as symbols of the United Kingdom's creativity, inventiveness, and focus on the future.' There was in fact very little about the Dome that was British. It was built by a Japanese company based in the United States.

Tony Blair also wrote: 'Throughout 2000, the Dome will inspire, entertain and educate all who visit, providing a once-in-a-lifetime experience.'

For some more than others ...

New Year's Eve 1999 was a disappointment for many in London. The British Airways Millennium Eye was declared unsafe. The £1 million 'River of Fire' failed to ignite properly. Transport to and from the scene of the London celebrations was almost nonexistent, and a combination of breakdowns in security at the Dome and administration in the Department for Culture, Media and Sport meant that more than 2,500 irate VIP invitees, in dinner suits and evening gowns, queued in the cold for up to seven hours. The Group 4 security guards struggled to cope with the chaos. The day before, the then Culture Secretary, Chris Smith, admitted that the sending out of Dome tickets had not been 'the smoothest of operations'. He was subsequently branded the 'Minister for Fiascos'.

Prince Charles delivered the first 'Thought for the Day' of the millennium on BBC Radio 4's *Today* programme. In a message that dwelled on religious and spiritual themes, the prince said: 'The millennium provides us with an opportunity to abandon the poles of blind optimism on the one hand and total despair on the other, and to rediscover a much older emotion – hope.'

The Dome's organizers spent most of the millennium year hoping for a miracle.

For many visitors, queuing became the symbol of the Dome. The British are famous for waiting patiently in queues, and people found themselves queuing for hours for Dome 'experiences' that lasted barely five minutes. Much attention focused on the apparent paradox that attendance figures were lower than expected but waiting times for the amusements inside the Dome were high.

In addition, many people were outraged at its £758 million cost, which eventually spiralled to £1.024 billion of public money – £180 million of which was provided in the form of special grants to make up for dismal ticket sales. The rest came from National Lottery 'good causes' money. The newspapers carried stories of NHS patients lying on trolleys in hospital corridors as the service ground almost to a halt for lack of funds. Five massive, fully equipped hospitals could have been built with the Dome money, or it would have paid the wages of five thousand NHS staff for ten years. It was easy to make a £758 million tent in Greenwich look like a waste of money.

An average of 17,153 people a day visited the Dome during Easter week; less than half the 35,000 capacity that the attraction's chief executive, Pierre-Yves Gerbeau, had hoped to create by introducing longer opening hours. By April the Dome was looking like it could fall 2 to 3 million visitors short of its target of 12 million. Eventually, just under 6 million people made the trip to Greenwich. Ten million paying visitors went to the 1951 Festival of Britain in only six months.

But on 30 December 1999, with just twenty-four hours to go, the Dome was full of optimism and what one observer called 'Dunkirk spirit' as exhibitors and showpeople desperately tried to get everything ready on time. It looked like a large trade fair running behind schedule, with piles of rubbish everywhere, but, miraculously, everything was ready inside the Dome on the big night.

One hour into the Millennium Dome's opening ceremony (at two minutes before midnight on 31 December 1999), the Queen opened the royal box and eight children ran down towards the central area to pull on large yellow ribbons that lowered giant curtains that shrouded the stage. Then, for a few seconds, the Dome was in darkness. Suddenly, a laser pierced the 203-carat De Beers Millennium Star diamond. The beam was split and refracted into thousands of points of light. Two children from the chorus walked towards the sparkling diamond. As they cupped their hands to figuratively extinguish the light, they began to sing 'A New Beginning' by modern classical British composer John Tavener. The song ended as the midnight chimes of Big Ben were piped into the Dome via a fibre-optic sound relay while the famous face of Parliament's timekeeper was projected on to cinema screens. The Millennium Star had been the focal point of the live event of the millennium, broadcast to millions of homes across the world. As far as De Beers were concerned, their £2 million had been well spent.

But the Oppenheimers might have reconsidered their decision had they been fully aware of where exactly their most precious diamonds were being kept.

3 – LOCATION, LOCATION, LOCATION

'Up in North London we have blue plaques to commemorate where famous people lived. Down in South London they instead have those yellow boards – you know, murder, stabbing, rape, appeal for witnesses, that kind of thing.'

BBC RADIO 4 PUNDIT ARTHUR SMITH

The East End is seen as the 'friendly face' of crime, with films, books and television programmes displaying the criminal fraternity as 'rough diamonds' who abide by a criminal code. East End gangsters were tough but fair (no one mugged a little old lady on the Krays' manor), charismatic and sometimes glamorous, attracting celebrities and gossip columnists alike. Recent books spawned by retired East End gangsters reinforce these ideas, as does the national press. The *Sun* newspaper was never able to resist the criminal allure of the Krays. It ran a story some years after Reggie Kray had been imprisoned for his part in the murder of fellow criminal and all-round nasty piece of work Jack 'the Hat' McVitie. It featured a photograph, smuggled out of prison, showing Reggie enjoying a cup of tea. The headline read: 'I Could Murder a McVitie!'

South London has a colder reputation when it comes to crime and outdoes the East End in every negative crime statistic there is. The reasons for this are historical. In the thirteenth century, Southwark Cathedral became a favoured place of sanctuary for those fleeing the city's justice. London's original prison, the 'Clink', was built in South

London, and by the seventeenth century there were seven jails south of the Thames. Despite these fearful prisons, where twenty people could be left suffocating overnight in a 6-by-6-foot pit, South Londoners remained the most criminally active and provided the city's authorities with more riot and disorder than they could handle.

For centuries, South London remained relatively unknown to other Londoners except as a source of disquiet. In the words of London writer Benedict le Vay: 'Southwark was where all the things the city could not tolerate but could not live without were sent.' North London would dump its dirt and rubbish on the South Bank of the Thames. It became a home to the 'stink' industries, which had been forced out of the main city. The tanneries were in Bermondsey; Lambeth housed vinegar makers, dye manufacturers and makers of soap and tallow. Gravediggers worked Lambeth, excavating bodies for 'candles of the fat, bone meal and dog's meat'.

The original Dog and Duck Tavern, located where the path of St George's Fields meets Lambeth Road, was famous for its prostitutes and said to be the 'most dreadful place in the metropolis' by its snooty northern neighbours. The highwaymen of the 1780s would drink at the Dog and Duck before meeting whores, fans or lovers by their horses in St George's Fields. Highwaymen were much admired by South Londoners, and many became the first 'commoners' to achieve celebrity status.

By 1800 Lambeth was a fully fledged slum, but it continued to grow. The construction of the Southwark, Waterloo and Vauxhall bridges led to massive house-building projects south of the river. Glue factories added to the already pungent smells, which varied from street to street. Odours of beer, jam, vinegar, leather and dung accompanied people as they waded to work through streets full of rubbish and slime.

The population explosion that occurred in the first part of the nineteenth century pushed a tidal wave of people south. Fields shrank and then vanished as businesses spread to Newington, Kennington and Walworth, and by the 1830s the basic structure of the South London we know today was pretty much established.

The East End provided a more intense kind of community than the South; there were more markets and music halls, for example. The Thames isolated the south, making it a desolate place to North Londoners, who even today would never dream of moving 'south of the river'. Radio 4 pundit Arthur Smith made this north–south snobbery very clear: 'Up in North London we have blue plaques to commemorate where famous people lived. Down in South London they instead have those yellow boards – you know, murder, stabbing, rape, appeal for witnesses, that kind of thing.'

The Thames was and still is a natural dividing line. The London Underground barely crosses the river. The Victoria Line makes it as far as Brixton, the Northern Line dips down as far as Morden, the Bakerloo to Elephant and Castle, the District to Richmond, and now, since 2000, the Jubilee Line stretches through Greenwich to Lewisham. Those few lines that cross the Thames on the London Underground map are but a handful of strands of spaghetti hanging over the edge of an overflowing bowl.

In the twenty-first century, South-East London is still the most crime-ridden area of the capital. In 2000 the boroughs of Southwark and Lambeth, immediately south of the Thames, were consistently numbers one and two in the crime league tables. They were only occasionally pipped to first place by Westminster as criminals popped across the river to target the toffs in the north (as well as naive tourists). For the financial year 2000–2001, Southwark was number one for murders at fourteen, Lambeth number two at thirteen. For crimes that involved violence against another person, Westminster was number one at 8,483, number two was Lambeth at 7,904, and number three was Southwark at 7,442.

Lambeth and Southwark are also the robbery capitals of London. Lambeth held the number-one spot for muggings, at 4,369. The nearest contender, Haringey, barely had half as many. Lambeth and Southwark were number one and two for robberies from banks, off-licences, shops, bookies, etc., with 322 and 214 respectively. According to the Metropolitan Police, London gangs commit three-quarters of all armed robberies that take place outside the capital, and 60 per cent of all armed robberies in Britain take place in the capital.

In the twenty-first century robbery ('blagging' to the initiated) makes peanuts in comparison with the rest of organized crime in Britain. In 1999 £2.5 million was netted in planned heists. For comparatively small rewards, robbing is a risky business. Firearms were used in 220 attacks, and 103 people were injured. This is but a tiny fraction of the money involved in organized crime. With a conservative estimate of £10 billion a year profit (some say the real figure is between £20 billion and £40 billion), organized crime is Britain's fourth largest industry. Most of the money comes from drugs and other smuggled goods, including cigarettes, alcohol and computer chips. More heroin is seized in the UK each year than in any other country in Europe. Londoners, Chinese, Japanese, Turkish, South American, Russian, Middle Eastern and Indian gangs battle it out in the capital for their slice of this multibillion-pound cake.

South London has been considered poor and disreputable for centuries, and its reputation as a dumping ground has stuck. These days, however, there are some positive changes afoot. The South Bank now houses a plethora of galleries and museums, pubs, new Thames-side flats and businesses. And in 2000 there was the Millennium Dome. Misguided as it turned out to be, the Dome was supposed to be beneficial for South London as it was intended to rejuvenate the area of Greenwich and the surrounding boroughs by creating jobs and affordable homes.

The Millennium Collection was supposed to bring some glamour to the Dome exhibition. While this may have been the case, South-East London has the highest proportion of criminals in the country. So putting the world's most valuable diamonds in a tent in Greenwich was equivalent to dangling the biggest carrot ever in front of a herd of hungry donkeys.

One of them was going to take a bite.

4 – THE GLIMMER OF AN IDEA

'It was the chance of a lifetime.'

RAY BETSON, DIAMOND GEEZER

Ray Betson, leader of the Diamond Geezers, was born on 6 September 1961 and grew up on the Walworth Road in South-East London. His early life was difficult and unsettled; his parents separated while he was a young boy and he lived with his mother. She was often ill, and this meant that he was passed from pillar to post.

Despite this, he remains good-humoured and charismatic. Betson is intelligent and a keen conspiracy theorist, believing that Masonic lodges rule a large part of society. He also believes that the police investigation of the Diamond Geezers is rife with subterfuge. Betson's voice is deep and earnest and his arguments are, for the most part, rationally put. Tall, bulky, muscle-bound, dark-haired and ruggedly handsome, he is every inch a South Londoner and a natural leader. Betson gives the impression that if he were able to follow orders he would succeed in the army. He is the kind of man who would lead a group of men on a mission and do his utmost to get them out in one piece. But if he didn't succeed, his conspiracy-led thinking would mean he would look for anyone or anything to blame for his failure. Not his men, to whom he would be completely loyal, but to some mysterious force.

Crime was always going to be his natural career choice. At school, his dyslexia meant that he was immediately seen as a stupid, troublesome pupil. He was drawn into mixing with truants and started to take part in petty crime, such as shoplifting. He was first arrested for theft at fourteen. By 1999 thirty-eight-year-old Ray Betson had served two eighteen-month jail sentences and had eighteen convictions, mainly for petty theft and vehicle offences, although nothing violent.

He lived the life of a true criminal, where it was a case of 'us and them' from birth, 'them' being the police. 'It was normal to be surrounded by stolen goods as we grew up,' said Betson. 'To me, there was nothing wrong with it; it was just a different kind of business to the normal sort. There was the added risk and danger of getting caught and the excitement of getting away with it. "Going away" is just part of life; it's like serving abroad if you're in the army.' While prison doesn't frighten most career criminals, the majority have no urge to become subject to Her Majesty's Pleasure any sooner than is absolutely necessary. Although a prison sentence means that they've 'earned their stripes', having the ironic bonus of making them more trustworthy to other criminal associates, many criminals get caught for things they needn't have.

The young Betson had seen how a pair of local blaggers, the Brinks Mat robbers Mickey McAvoy and Brian Robinson, had blown their golden fortune and were caught as a result. The police, not unnaturally, became suspicious when they moved from small South-East London council flats to large country houses in Kent (paid for in cash) and bought two Doberman guard dogs, which they named 'Brinks' and 'Mat'. As a young man, Betson was mentored by a successful career criminal, who steered him into the 'right kind of crime', the non-violent but profitable 'money crimes', such as fraud. He was warned against risking all in a 'one-hit wonder' crime such as Brinks Mat, which attracted so much attention that the authorities would never rest until the gold was recovered and the perpetrators were imprisoned, and then for a lengthy period. This meant that he was not a big enough fish to warrant too much attention from the police, or receive too long a sentence if caught. Betson was certain then that he wasn't going to make the same mistake as the Brinks Mat gang and kept his 'work' low-profile. Sometimes, though, a more serious criminal would ask him for a favour, to store something 'hot', for example. In the criminal world of South London, there is an unwritten rule that these favours cannot be refused: 'This is often more trouble than it's worth,' said Betson, 'as you can end up attracting attention from the police, who then get the wrong idea about you.' But apart from making a living from the proceeds of crime, the life of the Betson family was distinctly average. He met his present partner, Susan Foster, nine years ago, and together they have two young children. At the start of 1999 they were comfortably off; the money that Ray brought in was something akin to the wage of a supermarket manager. The problem was, of course, that what he did was illegal.

After some success in cheque fraud, Betson decided to use his capital to enter the profitable world of duty-free cigarette and alcohol smuggling. About £7 of the retail price of a bottle of whisky and about £4 (about 80 per cent) of the price of a packet of cigarettes is tax, so this was a trade in which substantial profits were to be made. It attracted Betson because this crime is very common and is treated leniently in the UK. It's a type of crime that gives a lot of law-abiding people exactly what they want: cheap cigarettes and drink. At least one person in every office up and down the country knows someone who does a 'Dieppe run', or has a van in which they do a 'weekend run' to Dieppe or Calais themselves. Fines are relatively light and prison sentences a rarity.

Raids are an occupational hazard. Naturally, Betson wasn't covered by any insurance when he lost a lot of money and stock (140,000 cigarettes) in two Customs and Excise raids at Dover in late 1999 and early 2000. 'About £16,000 each time,' he said ruefully (although the press reported figures between £50,000 and £160,000). Betson was the victim of a new government initiative: an investment of £209 million had just been made specifically to tackle tobacco smuggling, providing Customs with a thousand more officers as well as a new national network of the latest X-ray scanners. 'In 2000 I needed to make a lot of cash fast. I was in serious financial difficulties.' Because Betson couldn't pay his bills and was out of investment capital, he was tempted to look for a quick fix to get him back on track. This is often the primary motivating factor for the one-off type of crime favoured by robbers who need urgently to raise a stake. Typically, this type of criminal is young, brash and confident: he wants to get cash together in a hurry to invest in the profitable world of drug dealing, or to pay off debts. But this was not Betson. He had a very different kind of ambition, one of escape from grimy South-East London to the sunny climate of Marbella, the 'Costa del Crime', where successful Brit crims (many on the run from the law) seek luxurious sanctuary. Typically, the location ladder of the successful South London criminal starts with a move out of the relatively poverty-ridden areas of Rotherhithe, Bermondsey and Lambeth to the country lanes of Kent, where Betson lived, known as the 'Kent corridor'. The next step is to head for the Costa del Crime and, if you are particularly successful, the more salubrious parts of Marbella. Marbella has played home to numerous criminal expats since the 1970s. It is an idyllic existence, as criminals can plough their ill-gotten gains into legal investments and make a comfortable living as a result. It has become so popular that British food dominates the supermarkets – the only things from England these bandits on the run appear to miss are PG Tips and Wall's sausages.

Betson had a good friend, who, thanks to the London property boom, had made a packet and settled down in Puerto Banús, the upmarket part of Marbella. Betson had ideas about joining him, escaping the South London criminal fraternity with his family for a new and better life abroad in this British criminal ghetto. The problem was that, thanks to Customs, he didn't have enough money for the plane tickets, let alone a place to stay. When the Dome job cropped up, it was a case of right place, right time for Betson.

During the subsequent trial, Betson made the remarkable

allegation that his policeman 'brother-in-law' Michael Waring approached him with the idea of robbing the Dome in May 2000. Waring's wife was Betson's partner's sister. Although Waring eventually became godfather to one of Betson's children, they were reluctant relations to start with. When giving evidence Betson said: 'I dodged family gatherings as much as I could because my understanding was that Waring knew I was a criminal.' There was only so much dodging that Betson could do, however, and altogether they met about twenty times in five or six years. Betson said: 'On one family occasion just before Christmas 1996, Michael asked if I could get hold of some cheap booze and a leather jacket for his wife. I was a bit cagey, but he said: "You mustn't think me a fool." I asked him what he was talking about. Michael said that a friend of his at work had made some investigations and had found out that I was a fraudster. He said: "I don't worry about that. I leave the job at the office." And that broke the ice between us.

'I supplied him with what he asked for [Waring denies all of Betson's allegations, including that he ever received tobacco and cigarettes or anything else from Betson]. Then, just over a year later there was a Christmas get-together. Helen [Waring's wife] had apparently told Susan [Betson's partner] that Michael had been demoted from the CID, was very unhappy about this and thinking of leaving and getting a job in security. He said: "If you like, I could lose a load to you and you could take it off me." I thought it was a joke.

'He said: "Seriously, are you interested in anything like that?" And when I realized that he was serious, I had, at that time, no reason to get involved in this. I had good prospects from other crimes ... I wasn't pally-pally with him, didn't go drinking with him or go to the football with him, but by 1997 our relationship was one of mutual trust, and I thought that he wasn't a sort of lily-white policeman.'

Waring, an affable, slightly overweight, dark-haired, middle-aged man, had a good record as a Metropolitan Police constable. He had been awarded the Good Conduct Medal, an award for bravery, and was commended for tackling a man with a knife when off duty. He had been promoted to detective but claimed that the work didn't agree with him. He returned to work as a PC and was posted to patrol the perimeter of the Dome in November 1999 and stayed until July 2000. Waring had nothing to do with the day-to-day running of security at the Dome, although he had seen inside Bronze Control, the Dome's security office. There was never a shred of credible evidence, however, to suggest that Waring was other than honest and the judge made a point of making this clear during the trial.

Nevertheless, Betson claimed during the trial that he first discussed the idea to steal the diamonds from the Dome with Waring on 27 May 2000, which was also his son's birthday. Betson's and Waring's children were playing together while the two men walked and talked in the Strand, a local park. 'Waring told me: "I've got something which might interest you. I'm working at the Dome as part of the perimeter security." He claimed that he was working on a plan with an old school friend called Tony who was working at the Dome as a Group 4 security guard. Tony said that four or five people on the Dome staff had been straightened out [i.e. they were bent or, in other words, in on the plan].' Waring said this meeting did not occur and strenuously denies that he knew the Tony to whom Betson referred.

Betson continued: 'These people can effectively provide good service and act as lookouts. He said that some valuable stones were in the Dome and that he had got a plan together and got a backer, someone who wanted to buy the jewels.' Betson said that the buyer had promised a reward of £500,000 for the diamonds.

'He said security was crap. Police were not allowed to go in without approval of some senior police officer, and they were only allowed to patrol the outside. He and Tony had worked out a plan which involved a JCB.'

Betson said: 'Michael gave me confidence with regard to Tony. He said he could get plans and snippets of information. All I knew about Tony was what Michael told me. Michael said he used to go to school with him. I understood he had been sacked [from his job at the Dome] in late February, early March. He said he stayed in touch with the people who worked there. I trusted Tony to get involved in what I got involved in because of my relationship with Mike.

'He said he could provide us with help and that he could offer a period when nobody was about. I had every confidence in him, and I was very interested. I told Michael that I wanted to meet Tony, and it was arranged for us to meet in a pie-and-mash shop. Prior to this, I had gone to see Terry Millman for advice.'

Having had no experience of organized heists, Betson had approached an experienced criminal by the name of Terence Millman for help after the idea to steal the De Beers Millennium Collection was born. Millman jumped at the chance to be part of criminal history. Millman was a well-known 'face' in South London crime circles, an old pro with plenty of good contacts. He was the only one of the Diamond Geezers who had been convicted of serious armed robbery, having spent fourteen years in prison: 'Millman was a serious career criminal. Now, *he* was violent,' said the infamous 1960s gangster Tony Lambrianou, who died in 2004. Lambrianou, with the Krays' backing, racketeered the north of Britain, paying a cut to Ronnie and Reggie Kray. Along with renowned ex-armed robber Freddie Foreman (now retired), he knew Millman well: 'I liked Terry,' said Foreman; 'known him for thirty years, good man, up for a laugh, good sense of humour.'

The oldest member of the Diamond Geezers, Terry Millman, was born in Lambeth in 1944. Tall, thin and with a face full of deep laughter lines, he was a lifelong criminal and had been involved in a wide variety of robberies. Although Freddie Foreman speaks in favourable terms of Millman, he added: 'I was surprised to hear he was still at it at his age. I mean, nearly sixty: well, you know, he's getting on a bit.'

Over the years, Millman had taken part in all sorts of capers with people like Foreman and Lambrianou. Whether it was knocking off a lorry transporting cigarettes or blagging a jeweller, Millman was up for it. He seemed to be part of gangland legend, and had more than his share of tales to tell. As one former associate said: 'Terry was always getting himself into scrapes. Once, when he was a youngster, he had done a stick-up at this big off-licence in Morden. The guy put up a bit of resistance, but Terry came away with quite a few notes, a pretty good score. Problem was, he got back to his car and found he'd locked himself out! Next thing, he makes his getaway on foot, but now the guy from the off-licence is following him down the road screaming blue murder. Terry spots this car parked at the side of the road, engine running, guy in the driver's seat. Terry leaps in, waves the gun and tells him to drive. Problem is, the guy's a mechanic [who had been fixing the car] and the car only goes a hundred yards before the engine blows up! The guy from the off-licence catches up and won't leave Terry alone despite Terry threatening him with a shooter, so Terry has to give the money back and the bloke lets Terry go home empty-handed.'

'Terry was always telling tall stories,' said another ex-associate. 'He said that if he made a big score he would give some money to his missus because she was a "good girl" and had put up with a lot of his nonsense. He told me that a few years back the police had come looking for him at home and asked his missus to confirm his description. She said that he was dark, broad and handsome, faithful, good to the kids, tall, with kind, clear eyes. When the policeman said, "That's not the description we have here," she replied, "Well, if you can find me someone like that, can you bring him here and keep Terry?"'

So what drove Millman to take on such a risky job at an age where he should have been thinking about retirement? There was a reason, a much deeper one than the usual dream of earning a quick buck. Millman was suffering from terminal cancer of the stomach and wasn't having treatment. He knew he did not have long to live. He was in constant pain and would drink to ease it. The chance to steal the Millennium Star was, quite literally for Millman, to die for. It appealed to his sense of humour and gave him a chance to go down in history. He had been looking for a 'big score' so that he could go out with a bang and had already made at least one failed robbery attempt in 2000 (the security van in Aylesford). If the theft of the Millennium Collection came off, Millman would be able to enjoy whatever time he had left to the full.

Millman was known among the criminal fraternity for his cheeky humour. Despite the terrible, constant pain of his cancer, he always had a smile on his face. Even at the trial, Judge Michael Coombe kept referring to him as 'Merriman' and had to apologize for making this continuous reference: 'I am told that more than once – in fact every time – I managed to call him Merriman. I apologize if it was in any way misleading.' But Millman was no pussycat. One ex-colleague said that Millman was prepared to use violence and was 'not afraid to use a gun'. Betson, acutely aware of this, said: 'When I first met Terry, I said we were not going to be carrying any weapons. Terry said we'd have to see that the plan was foolproof but agreed in principle. I arranged to go with Terry to meet Tony.

'Tony said he had four or five of the Dome staff who were going to be complicit with us. He said he would get overalls, uniforms and identity cards and get plans to the cabinets and keys as well. He would make sure that there would be no resistance, and we would simply come in, steal the jewels and go. Tony said that he had a buyer for the jewels and they were worth hundreds of thousands of pounds.' A slight underestimation, but perhaps Tony was referring to what they would be worth to Betson.

'I knew then that I would need at least three or four people to carry it out. Tony also asked me to find a safe house, somewhere to put a JCB and anything else we would need, including a boat.'

Betson continued: 'Tony had given us a lot of thinking to do, and Terry and I talked about the proposal and kept it to ourselves. We talked to no one else at that early stage, but we thought it was a good plan.'

Arrangements were then made to meet in a public library a week later, where Tony showed Betson and Millman the blueprints of the Dome and the vault, and supplied Betson with a mobile phone so that they could stay in direct contact.

'Tony expanded on the plan,' said Betson. 'He described how we should use a JCB. We would go to a point on an approach road, near a side entrance to the Dome, where we would wait until one of the bent Dome staff would coordinate with me by walkie-talkie. There was a gap in the fence where we could drive through, but there was a small concrete bollard in the way. The JCB was going to take care of it. The idea to use a JCB seemed reasonable because there was loads of work going on in the area at the time. Tony said that a van as opposed to a JCB would look suspicious and that no one would be expecting a raid using a JCB. It seemed plausible.' JCBs were working in and around the Dome throughout 2000, building and repairing exhibits, carrying heavy items and so on.

'After the raid, we'd go through a gap in the fence up the approach road and head for the beach by the *Slice of Reality*.' A *Slice of Reality* is a piece of artwork by Richard Wilson: a 25-foot-wide cross-section through the bridge of a small coaster, sitting on the mud next to a small beach by the Dome. It is still there today. 'The boat would pick us up there. At no stage did the use of force cross my mind. We were going to be straight in and straight out. It was a simple smash-and-grab job. I understood there would be members of the public in the plaza area, but not in the approach to the vault,' Betson explained. 'We were told that Group 4 security would not get there. There was no real possibility that they might. If overwhelming force did appear, we would have to give up.'

Betson decided it was now time to recruit the rest of the Diamond Geezers and develop a concrete, fail-safe plan.

5 – THE DIAMOND GEEZERS

'I thought it was pie in the sky.'

BILL COCKRAN, DIAMOND GEEZER

Having decided that the job was doable and that the risks were worth the £500,000 reward promised by the buyer, Betson started his recruitment drive. By September, two months before their final attempt, the Diamond Geezers were almost fully formed.

They were an unusual collection, consisting of a combination of age and experience and youth and audacity. Each of the four core members of the gang came from within the criminal world of South-East London, and each was born in a different decade. Between them, they had sixty years of criminal experience to draw on, even if nearly all of it was strictly small time. But for the members of the Diamond Geezers it was, as Bill Cockran put it, simply a question of: 'Do we stay small time, or do we go for the big time?'

The 'ringleader' of the gang, naturally, was thirty-eight-year-old Ray Betson. His role was to drive a JCB through the perimeter fence into the Dome and out again, taking three passengers and the diamonds to meet the getaway boat. It would also have to ram a bollard that was in the way of the gate they were planning to enter by, and the JCB's bucket was the ideal tool for the job.

Betson said: 'We [Betson and two other gang members, Ciarrocchi and Cockran] went to the Dome and checked out the gate nearest to the De Beers vault. We saw that there was a gap in the fence, which we got through, then a blue gate, and finally we strolled into the Dome through a large corrugated shutter door. On all occasions when I went, the shutter was open. I thought this looked ridiculously easy. We went and looked at the jewel exhibition. There was a host outside, but the arrangement was with Tony that when we went in there would not be anybody outside who was not on our side. We then walked to the *Slice of Reality*, where there is a beach. Having inspected the Dome, we thought it was the opportunity of a lifetime.'

Betson decided to recruit an old friend as his second-in-command. William Thomas Cockran was born on 24 October 1952. He was overweight but strong, having worked in the building trade. For a while he ran his own firm and did a variety of odd jobs such as furniture delivery. Married with two children, the fair-haired Cockran had previous convictions for petty crime, but again there was no record of anything violent. He was fearlessly loyal to Betson. Cockran wasn't perhaps as bright as Ray but he was up for anything his friend was.

Cockran, who had grown up with the younger Betson on the Walworth Road, said: 'I thought it was pie in the sky at first, a joke, but he had inside help,' and said during the trail: 'I was a bit dubious, but I thought we could trust him [referring to Waring], being a member of the family. Waring said it was a piece of cake. I could not believe how simple it was from what he told me. My reward would be £70,000, which went up to £100,000 later on.

'I visited [the Dome] two or three times to look around and see how true it was, what was going on. I could not believe the security was so bad and that there was no one in the vault.'

Cockran's job was to find a way to smash the glass and get the diamonds out of the vault. 'When in the vault, I examined the glass and tapped it. My skill was to break into cabinets and I knew a way. I am in the building trade and have had burglary experience. The Hilti gun was my idea, as was the sledgehammer.' A Hilti gun is a builder's tool that with one explosive punch blasts nails of any length into almost any material, saving builders the repeated use of a hammer. Cockran was sure that this would simultaneously crack and heat up the protective glass so much that someone using a heavy sledgehammer would be able to smash a hole straight through in under a minute.

'I had to find out about the alarm system. From what I could see, I knew it would take a long time for the police to get there. I appreciated people would respond to the alarm, but I estimated that it would take about four to five minutes for Group 4 to get there, which was longer than we needed.'

Next on the list was fifty-five-year-old Terry Millman. He used his connections to help set up the raid, but on the day Betson made sure he was well away from the action: 'Millman was up for going into the Dome,' said Betson, 'but what with his illness and record for armed robbery, I thought it best that he be as far away as possible and so made sure he was the second van driver, on the other side of the river.'

His job was driving the getaway van that would be waiting for the speedboat on the north side of the Thames.

The fourth member of the Diamond Geezers was Italian Aldo Ciarrocchi, at twenty-nine years old 'the kid' of the gang. He was born on 16 September 1969 and grew up in South-East London with Cockran and Betson. He was brought up by an Italian father and British mother on a South London council estate and left school with few qualifications, preferring to live by his wits. 'I've known Bill [Cockran] for a very long time, and Betson all my life,' he said. 'I was going out with Bill's oldest daughter when I met him.' When Ciarrocchi and Cockran's daughter went through a rough patch and separated after six years, Cockran and Ciarrocchi became close friends.

After leaving school, Ciarrocchi picked up what casual work he could and became involved in petty crime. He was caught shoplifting and received a short jail sentence. He made quite an impression while inside as a gifted listener and talker. He actually counselled fellow inmates as a member of the prison Samaritans. After his release from jail, Ciarrocchi set up a property company and was flying high in 1998 when he met Elisabeth Kirsch, a twenty-five-year-old American model and English Literature student.

Elisabeth was at that time taking six months off from her university studies to work as a model in Paris and London. Her waif-like body and delicate face were exactly in keeping with the fashion of the time, so Kirsch had no shortage of work or admirers. But she didn't enjoy her time in Paris and felt lonelier still in London. After two miserable weeks in the city she decided to telephone Aldo, whose name had been given to her by a friend. 'Although it was quite difficult for me to understand his heavy cockney accent, we clicked straight away and talked for an hour. He told me to call him if I needed anything.' She called two days later asking him to help her move flats. They met by the phone boxes at Tower Hill tube station. 'I didn't know what to expect,' she said, 'but I knew it was him as soon as I saw him. He had really dark hair and was wearing dark sunglasses, a black shirt and black trousers. He looked like a movie star. He took me back to his Docklands flat in one of the marinas. He didn't make a pass at me, but something immediately clicked between us. He then spent four hours helping me move.' They met again a couple of days later. Aldo maintained his 'movie star' image by telling Kirsch that he had four other girlfriends and didn't want to get involved.

In his expensive suit, shades and Saab, he was constantly drawing admiring glances from other women, as Kirsch could see, and after a while they became committed lovers. But what Kirsch didn't know then was that Ciarrocchi's car was rented, as was his Docklands flat, that he wasn't seeing another four women and nor was his business flying quite as high as he made out. Ciarrocchi had fallen for Kirsch and was pulling out all the stops to impress this highbrow American model, and while doing so he was letting his business slip into debt.

When Elisabeth returned to New York after their first few meetings, the lovers spoke on the telephone for about three hours every day and, over the following months, visited each other when they could. She moved in with him in London in August 1999, following her graduation from New York University. Initially, she couldn't have been happier.

'We got on like a house on fire,' she beams. 'He always behaved like a complete gentleman to me. He has never been rough or hit me. In fact he said he wanted to be my knight in shining armour and give me everything. He is so romantic. He would suddenly ask me if I fancied fish and chips, then whisk me off to Brighton in his Saab to buy some. He would hide sweets under my pillow and prepare surprise treats like strawberries and cream.'

But Ciarrocchi's property business went bust in early 2000. He tried setting up a slot-machine company, but the competition was tough and sometimes violent. It didn't pay nearly as well, and he was struggling to cope financially. To make matters worse, he had just splashed out on an expensive Cartier watch for Kirsch. Ciarrocchi was madly in love with this beautiful model and was constantly preoccupied with the fear that if he failed to maintain his high-flying lifestyle he would lose the love of his life.

To try to raise some extra money, he took to helping out Betson with the cashing of stolen and forged traveller's cheques, but soon Ciarrocchi found that he was without an income and unable to pay his bills. Then Betson told him that he 'might have something to get [him] out of trouble; something has come up'. A few days after Cockran, Betson and Ciarrocchi met in a shopping centre to discuss the crime, Cockran called him to ask if he 'was still going to the party'.

'At first I was a bit shocked, but once I understood what was going to happen I agreed to be involved,' he said. Like Betson, Ciarrocchi had plans to escape South London, but instead of Marbella he wanted to start a new life in America with Kirsch. The Dome raid would provide plenty of capital for this.

The police had no intelligence on Ciarrocchi other than his previous conviction for shoplifting. He was allotted two roles on the day. He was to monitor police frequencies to make sure they were not being followed and then set off smoke and stink bombs outside the diamond vault to keep the public away and cause maximum confusion.

The police thought that the driver of the getaway boat would be forty-eight-year-old James Hurley. Betson said in court that he had known the fair-haired and ruggedly handsome Hurley for twenty years but has since refused to say anything else about him. Detective Chief Superintendent Jon Shatford, who led the operation to catch the gang, said: 'I don't think he had any form whatsoever. He was known by us as a "name", as being "around" the gang, but we knew nothing more than that.' Even the friends and associates of the Diamond Geezers knew little about Hurley except that he had some property in South London.

Completing the line-up of the Diamond Geezers was, of course, the man who supposedly planned it all, Tony. He was the mysterious 'inside man' who, according to Betson, 'looked a bit like Vinnie Jones'. They first met in a pie-and-mash shop and then in a library, where, Betson said, Tony showed him and Cockran a blueprint of the Dome. Betson added that Tony claimed to have worked as part of the Dome's security and had a buyer for the jewels lined up.

The final plan was simple and made for a fast raid and getaway. 'I wasn't told an exact time,' said Betson, 'but we worked out that there would be a time delay because when the system was tripped it'd go straight through to Hatton Garden first and they'd notify the Dome. I believed that there wouldn't be any security anywhere around the outside of the millennium jewels – obviously, they had to come from Bronze Control [Dome security HQ] or the security compound. We calculated that it would take three to four minutes for the security to get there, and by that time we would be on the other side of the Thames. We were also told that Group 4 don't come up and directly intervene in any situation of a theft, or anything like that. They just call out the position over their radio and then it's dealt with by the police.'

At 9.25 a.m., Betson would drive a JCB down Millennium Way to the car park in front of Gate 4, which they had established from various visits was always open. This led to a part of the Dome's structure which was also always open, so the JCB would be able to drive straight inside and almost instantly be alongside the vault where the diamonds were being exhibited. The JCB would be specially modified so that it could carry Cockran and Ciarrocchi as passengers.

The gang would all carry walkie-talkies. Betson would wait on hearing the command to 'stand by' from Tony, and the raid would begin in earnest when the 'straightened-out' security guards inside were certain no one was around. Tony would then give the signal – 'Attack, attack! Attack, attack!' – at 9.30, the time chosen because, as Betson explained, the area outside the jewel house would be closed to the public until 9.30. 'There would not be any maintenance people about, and so it was safe to go in,' he said. The vault would be opened only at 9.30, and the tides were right for the escape route at this time. 'We were going to use the pier next to *A Slice of Reality*, nearest to Gate 10,' Betson said, 'and there we were going to use a beach where a boat would be available. We wanted to use that beach, but it depended on the tides.'

Betson would be wearing a latex mask over a balaclava on entering the Dome to hamper any later description of him from witnesses who might have seen him driving to the Dome. The mask had been bought from a joke shop and was supposed to be of Prime Minister Tony Blair, but from a distance and through the windshield of the JCB it looked relatively inconspicuous. 'A JCB driver wearing a gas mask would have looked a bit odd,' said Betson. The others would already be wearing gas masks. Once inside, Betson would remove the latex mask and put on his gas mask. These were worn to save them from the effects of the ammonia. They also acted as an additional means of disguise.

Once inside the Dome, Ciarrocchi would wait outside the vault and release his smoke bombs to create confusion as well as giving the gang some cover. Meanwhile, Cockran would weaken the glass cabinets with the Hilti gun and then smash holes through the glass with a sledgehammer (09.31).

Then they would cut the diamonds free of their stands with a set of bolt cutters, spray the glass display and floor with ammonia to contaminate DNA evidence (hair, perspiration, blood, fibres) and return to the waiting JCB (09.33). The gang would then head for the small beach by *A Slice of Reality* (09.34).

Hurley would be waiting in a speedboat and would whisk them across the Thames into Bow Creek. They would land the boat under Lower Lea Crossing (09.36) and make their way into Orchard Place, where Terry Millman would be in the getaway van.

They would then set off down the A1261, Aspen Way, through the Limehouse Link Tunnel that crosses back over the Thames into Southwark, which is, as the crow flies, three miles from the Dome. They would then zip round into Rotherhithe Street, a quiet cul-de-sac, and meet the mystery buyer at the Mayflower pub (10.15). The diamonds would be exchanged for cash, and then the gang would start to go on their separate ways. Less than an hour after the crime began, the Diamond Geezers would be 'in the clear' and £500,000 richer.

But it was never going to be that simple.

6 – THE LYING SQUAD

'Other criminals walked in fear of the name Ray Betson.'

DETECTIVE CHIEF SUPERINTENDENT JON SHATFORD

Chatham, Kent, 9.30 p.m., 7 July 2000. Betson was watching the discerning criminals' favourite programme, *Crimewatch UK*, when the phone rang. It was Terry Millman, fresh from the failure of the Aylesford robbery, keen as mustard, with no time to spare, and anxious to get on with the next job. They arranged to meet at Tong Farm.

Tong Farm is near Tunbridge Wells in Kent. It is a fairly nondescript place, if untidy. Its fields are littered with a variety of vehicles, including farm machinery and horseboxes. Despite its slightly run-down, unassuming appearance, Tong Farm is home to one of the most feared families in Kent. Locals describe the Wenhams as the 'neighbours from hell' and instinctively lower their voices when they talk about them. They arrived quite literally with a bang. James Wenham bought Tong Farm for £220,000 (paid in cash) in March 2000, but one tenant who lived in a small cottage just within its boundaries refused to move. He was suddenly persuaded when, without warning, Wenham literally bulldozed his home with a JCB. The Wenhams subsequently did their best to paint a picture of themselves as honest horse dealers. But one member of the family, James's son Lee, was already of interest to

Kent's Regional Crime Squad for vehicle theft and for handling stolen goods.

Detective Superintendent Andy Dolden, from Kent's Serious Crimes Unit, had been watching Lee Wenham for a while: 'We knew he had been dealing in stolen goods, but I had an idea that he was on to something bigger. As I knew he was a career criminal, I wanted to catch him at something serious so that we could put him away for a good few years.'

After rushing to the scene of the attempted robbery in Aylesford, Dolden recognized one of the vans used by the gang, which had been spotted by detectives at Tong Farm some weeks earlier. A quick countrywide check soon brought Dolden's attention to a raid that had occurred earlier in the year in Nine Elms in London, which, except for the Fray Bentos tins, was identical in its execution.

In Nine Elms, South London, in the early hours of a cold February morning in 2000 – a stone's throw from the famous landmark of Battersea Power Station and within earshot of Battersea Dogs' Home – one of the most dramatic attempted armed raids in British criminal history took place.

As a Securicor van carrying £10 million in cash turned into a Battersea side street, a remarkable trap was sprung. First, three lorries were driven into position in nearby streets, cutting off any route into the area and any route out for the Securicor van should it have tried to escape. Then, a BMW saloon shot out of a junction and screeched across the van's path, forcing the driver to a stop. Four men leaped out of the BMW, and five more piled out of the back of a large blue Transit van parked just opposite. Two were carrying shotguns. One ran up to a 7-ton lorry fitted with a spike parked further up the street and positioned directly behind the security van, and climbed inside.

Unfortunately, when parking 'Gertie' the lorry, the robbers had blocked off a parked car. The owner had returned to find his car trapped and, outraged at being blocked in, had taken the keys that had been left in Gertie's ignition in protest. Gertie's driver searched the cab frantically before patting his pockets in disbelief while his colleagues looked on incredulously. One of the gang cried out: 'It's the cozzers! Run!' Thinking the police were on to them, they aborted the mission and escaped in a speedboat moored near Battersea Power Station. The speedboat was later found burned out in Chelsea Harbour.

What made Dolden absolutely certain that it was the same gang that had committed both raids was that the ramming vehicle used in Nine Elms had been labelled 'Gertie'; the ramming vehicle in Aylesford had been named 'Gertie II', and on Gertie II Lee Wenham had scratched the words 'Persistent ren't [sic] we?' into the paint. Then, a ten-week forensic analysis revealed that saliva found on a pair of rubber gloves left on the dashboard in the van in Aylesford belonged to Lee Wenham. The police were also eventually able to establish that Millman was at the Aylesford robbery, thanks to a fingerprint found on a bucket inside the van. Although this linked them to the raid, it wasn't enough to secure a conviction for armed robbery, so it was a case of patiently watching and waiting, trying to see where the gang would strike next. With two unsuccessful attempts under their belt, Dolden felt that it would be only a matter of time.

Betson drove down to Tong Farm blissfully unaware that the Aylesford robbery attempt had taken place the day before. Once there, Terry Millman introduced Betson to thirty-three-year-old Lee Wenham. Although he would not be anywhere near the Dome on the day, Wenham played a crucial role. Wenham was the criminally minded mechanic behind Gertie and Gertie II. On Millman's suggestion, Wenham redesigned Betson's JCB so that it would be an effective ramming vehicle. He made it faster by removing some internal components and created enough room for a driver and three passengers. The boat, JCB and two vans used on the day of the Dome raid were stored at his family home, Tong Farm, which also became the Diamond Geezers' safe house. Prior to the attempt itself, the vehicles would be moved to a South London scrapyard run by associates of the Wenhams. The scrapyard was in Old Coal Yard in Plumstead, South-East London.

While Betson was getting out of the car and shaking Millman's hand, just over a mile away a camera shutter whirred and clicked half a dozen times, capturing the new arrival on film. As per Dolden's instructions, Tong Farm was, from that morning, being watched most attentively by a team of six detectives from Kent's Regional Crime Squad's specialist surveillance team. Each member of the gang observed by the team was given a codename. Betson's was Bracken.

If the theft of the millennium was going to succeed, the inexperienced trio of Betson, Cockran and Ciarrocchi had to rely on assistance from the mysterious Tony and his inside knowledge; Millman, who had the experience and connections; and Wenham, who had the means and the know-how to get them into the Dome. Thanks to his decision to involve Millman, Betson had been spotted by the police. The police made the mistaken but logical assumption that he was one of the Nine Elms/Aylesford gang and that anyone that Betson spent a lot of time with was also likely to have taken part in these armed robberies.

The police were expecting another raid on a Securicor van and had picked the Dartford branch as the next likely target, but they were about to learn that not only was Betson about to up the stakes, he was also going to try to set a new world record. This, of course, only reinforced his mistaken reputation as a serious blagger. Detectives were surprised when, shortly after Betson was first seen at Tong Farm, Wenham paid a visit to the Dome. Unable to follow closely enough, the detectives were not able to establish what exactly he was up to. When this was reported to Dolden, he authorized full-time surveillance of Betson, the new face on the scene, suspecting that he could be the link to the next job.

Detectives became more and more puzzled as a JCB arrived on the farm and Lee Wenham devoted several days to its maintenance. Then another new face appeared: James Hurley. Hurley went with Betson and Cockran to test-drive a speedboat. This made sense to the police. A speedboat fitted the Aylesford and Nine Elms *modus operandi*. Betson was followed to London, where he was also observed by dumbfounded detectives visiting the Dome. He went with Susan, his children and Cockran. The two men spent less time looking at the exhibits than at the actual structure and layout of the building. Except for one area, of course: the Money Zone, more specifically the De Beers diamond vault. The two men were observed at 11 a.m. on 1 September taking a long, almost reverential look at the diamonds. Cockran was seen tapping the glass, his nose pressed against the window like a boy outside Hamleys a week before Christmas. Betson and Cockran then took a walk outside the Dome, working their way towards a restricted area and videotaping potential escape routes while the police videotaped them. They met Ciarrocchi at 4 p.m. that same day at a Greenwich shopping centre and were again caught on the police video, talking animatedly, with much hand-waving by Ciarrocchi.

As word spread among the detectives from the Kent Regional Crime Squad that Betson and Wenham had been studying the diamond vault, the same question was asked again and again: 'Surely they can't be thinking of robbing the Dome?' Kent detectives had reluctantly alerted their colleagues from the Metropolitan Police to the potential raid on 21 August. They were reluctant because there is often a fear among different departments and divisions in the police that after a lot of hard work another branch gets the credit for the arrest. The rivalry between Kent and the Metropolitan Police forces is very strong, particularly as a number of South London criminals live in the so-called 'Kent corridor' so their operations are known to both forces. There can sometimes be an element of gang-like competition as to who exactly gets to take credit for the 'collar', especially as many South London criminals living in the Kent corridor do their dirty work in the capital. So when Met detective Jon Shatford first heard that his Kent colleagues thought the Dome was going to be the subject of a robbery attempt, he was pleased to get the tip-off. At the time, Shatford was a superintendent based at Scotland Yard. About 5 feet 10 with light brown/grey-white hair and no sign of middle-age spread, Shatford actually looks nowhere near his retirement age. He talks with a softly spoken, West Country voice, his eyes never leaving his subjects and his gaze never broken by a blink. One armed robber memorably describes his classic 'copper stare' as 'piss-holes in the snow'.

Shatford joined up when he was twenty-one: 'It's an exciting, different career, diverse and interesting; I developed an early passion from watching TV programmes such as Z-Cars and seeing policemen walking the beat. I had a number of jobs until I joined the Met, which is, of course, the biggest and most exciting section of the force.'

He was appointed operational head once he was fairly certain what the Diamond Geezers' objectives were. This meant he was solely responsible for the operation's successful execution and could draw on whatever resources the Met had available. He immediately decided to mobilize the entire Flying Squad, including its specialist surveillance team. 'This was roughly some time in August [2000], although I must say that this was a lot of speculation. But, yes, an inkling in August ... I suppose I was certain for the first time when Betson and Cockran were spotted at the Dome by surveillance officers on 1 September. When the file landed on my desk, I looked at it and thought this seems too incredible to believe,' said Shatford. 'It just didn't seem real.'

From the Kray twins to Kenneth Noye, the Flying Squad has been at the centre of British criminal investigations for over eighty years. The squad was formed by Detective Inspector David Goodwillie in 1919, as the 'Mobile Patrol Experiment', in response to growing concern about an influx of organized crime from overseas into the capital. Criminals dubbed it 'the heavy mob', and later 'the Sweeney Todd' (rhyming slang for Flying Squad), as it handled some of the Met's most high-profile cases, concentrating on armed robberies and organized crime. Officers conducted surveillance operations from the backs of two horse-drawn, canvas-covered Great Western Railway vans (perhaps not so different from officers hiding in the back of a Transit van today). The group's original twelve detectives were allowed to pursue criminals into any police division area. In 1920 the Daily Mail referred to this group as 'flying squads of hand-picked detectives' and the name stuck.

Flying Squad officers face considerable dangers. They are

specialists in the 'pavement ambush', swooping on armed robbers while they are committing a crime. Although their sheer speed usually wins the day, it is a high-risk form of policing and certainly not for the faint-hearted. In 2000 they foiled an attempted armed robbery on Barclays' Westminster branch. These highly trained specialists were armed with sub-machine guns and achieved conspicuous success. There was special praise for Police Constable John Benson, who shot himself in the groin as he jumped from a Land Rover to chase two of the suspects. 'He did a great job,' said Detective Superintendent Albert Patrick, no doubt with his tongue firmly placed in his cheek. Another recent high-profile success for the Flying Squad was the arrest of David Copeland, the Brixton nail bomber who killed three people and injured seventy when he blew up the Admiral Duncan pub in Soho in April 1999.

However, the Flying Squad had suffered a great deal of controversy in recent years, and the Dome caper could not have come at a better time. It was a welcome chance to distract from the corruption scandals that had dogged the squad. The unit's officers have always been chosen because of their knowledge of the underworld. Extensive contacts with paid informants have been the jewel in the crown of the squad's intelligence operations for years. The Flying Squad is unique in that it solves 40 per cent of its cases through informers. Other non-dedicated units solve only about 5 per cent of crimes this way. Sometimes, however, this close relationship with the criminal fraternity backfires, with truly disastrous consequences. The relationship between policeman and informer is open to abuse from both sides as detectives allow criminals to continue their careers uninterrupted in return for information. Kenneth Noye became an informer to get rid of the competition and led the Flying Squad straight to the doors of his rivals. Noye was eventually convicted for the road-rage murder of Steven Cameron, and had previously stabbed a policeman to death, although he was acquitted by a jury on the grounds of self-defence.

In February 1972 the head of the Flying Squad, Commander Kenneth Drury, was revealed to have just spent a two-week holiday in Cyprus with James Humphreys, one of seven porn barons named by the British press. Drury claimed they were looking for Ronnie Biggs, the escaped Great Train Robber. But on 7 July 1977 Justice Mars-Jones stated that Drury was the 'chief architect' behind the porn syndicate in Central London and sentenced him to eight years' imprisonment. Another twelve Scotland Yard detectives were jailed for accepting bribes.

For a time the unit was disbanded before resurfacing in the 1980s. By the 1990s the squad was linked to corruption once again. A purge was started by Sir Paul Condon, the former Metropolitan Police Commissioner, who estimated that up to 250 officers in the Met were corrupt. 'I believe that the overwhelming majority of the 27,000 men and women in the Met are honest, decent and brave,' he said. 'However, I do have a minority of officers who are corrupt, dishonest and unethical. They commit crimes, they neutralize evidence in important cases and they betray police operations and techniques to criminals.' It seemed that the majority of these corrupt policemen worked for the Flying Squad.

A breakthrough in corruption investigation came when two Flying Squad detectives, Terry McGuinness and Kevin Garner, became the first to break ranks in twenty years and turned supergrasses. They were big, tough policemen. McGuinness's nickname was 'Meathead', and he was a respected ex-amateur boxer who had sparred with Frank Bruno. They confessed to a series of charges after a sting set up by the Metropolitan Police's Complaints Investigations Bureau (CIB3) in December 1997. CIB3 officers planted eighty 1-kilogram bars of cannabis (police estimated the value at £250,000) inside a bathroom cabinet in an East London flat. After leaking information about the whereabouts of the haul, McGuinness and Garner were filmed stealing the drugs. They were arrested and charged. Soon after, McGuinness pleaded guilty and turned supergrass. Garner followed suit.

As a result, the homes and workplaces of a total of nineteen Flying Squad detectives, ranging in rank from detective constable to detective chief inspector, were searched. One former officer said:

'This is not some remote squad. It's the robbery squad, which is part of Scotland Yard's specialist operations department.' Eventually, 49 officers of a 125-strong team stood accused of corruption. Allegations included claims that detectives brokered financial deals with criminals or tipped them off about investigations. Some became involved with drug dealing. One criminal came forward and claimed that squad officers helped themselves to £3,500 from an armed raid he had carried out. Other accusations included the payment of rewards to people who were not entitled to them, and other bribes to officers for a range of favours, including taking confidential data from the Police National Computer.

McGuinness revealed the existence of a 'first-aid kit', which included a balaclava and an imitation gun, used to plant evidence on suspects. McGuinness also described how his unit raided a suspect's home and found £14,000 under a bed. Officers carried off the cash after the criminal invited them to take it with the words: 'Christmas has come early.'

As a result of the investigations by the CIB, several people have been freed from prison. East Londoners John 'Chainsaw Woody' Woodruff, sixty-three, and William 'Mad Dog' Hickson, fifty-six, were jailed for seveteen years for conspiracy to rob, robbery and possessing firearms at the Old Bailey in April 1997. They had been accused of robbing £33,000 from a post office in Manor Park, East London, in January 1996, armed with a handgun. The pair said that officers from the Flying Squad had planted a gun on them. They said they had been lured there after being told by Flying Squad detectives that cash would be given to them across the counter. The BBC's *Nine O'Clock News* found evidence, on videotape, supporting their claim that a gun had been planted on them. The film shows that the tape appears to have been cut because the timer jumps. A gun appears during the gap.

As can probably be told from their nicknames, these guys are no angels. They have (so far) been sentenced to a total of sixty years in prison for a series of multi-million-pound robberies. In the 1960s, Woodruff was jailed for twelve years for armed robberies with sawn-off shotguns. He was jailed again, in 1979, for eighteen years for his part in a robbery in Banstead, Surrey, in which an armed gang cut into a security van with a chainsaw and stole more than £1 million. Hickson was arrested after a £6 million robbery on a Security Express depot in 1983. He was jailed for six years.

If Woodruff and Hickson were the only ones who could prove that they were illegally entrapped by the Flying Squad, then perhaps the squad could claim this was exceptional, that this sort of thing didn't happen very often, and never to innocent people (after all, Chainsaw Woody and Mad Dog were lifelong criminals who were not about to become reformed characters, and many people would think that the Flying Squad were justified in using any means necessary to put them away for a long time). However, there are more. Many more.

McGuinness and Garner were involved in the wrongful arrest and conviction of Michael Brown, 27, Anthony Taylor, 29, and Kevin Martin, 30. They were each sentenced to ten years for raiding a jeweller's shop in Edmonton, North London, and stealing gems worth £6,000 after immobilizing the owner with a stun gun. In a scene more reminiscent of the Keystone Kops than the Flying Squad, Martin and his girlfriend were woken at 7.30 a.m. by bangs, crashes and shouts coming from next door. The police had smashed down his neighbour's door by mistake. Realizing their blunder, officers then trampled into Martin's flat. Martin said one of the officers turned to him and boasted he 'stitched up guys like [him] all day long'. The evidence, only produced seven months after the crime, was suspicious. On the first two occasions when prints were sent for analysis, the result was negative: they did not match Martin's. The detectives insisted on sending them for a third time and suddenly a positive match was found. At first, when Martin tried to complain that he had been fitted up, the officer from the complaints department said he believed him but added: 'No judge or jury will ever believe those officers fitted you up. You've just got to serve your sentence.' Seven months into Martin's sentence, his younger brother, Jason, committed suicide. The brothers had been close, and Jason had had a breakdown after Kevin's conviction. Eventually, Kevin

Martin was released on bail in June 2000 after a CIB3 investigation. He said: 'There's a lot of other guys in prison going through all this who have been fitted up, and no one's listening. I just want this to give all those people hope.'

In yet another case, George Ellis, 37, from Bethnal Green, East London, was serving fourteen years in prison for a £37,500 armed robbery when he was freed in 2000 by the Court of Appeal as a result of criminal charges brought against Flying Squad detectives. Ellis had claimed during his trial that a Flying Squad officer had planted false evidence against him.

Scotland Yard is so concerned about corruption that it has now employed a tactic previously used only on the general public. The 'Rat on a Rat' scheme has been adjusted for the Met; called 'the Right Line', it is a hotline for honest officers to report their suspicions. But it's not just the foot soldiers of the Flying Squad who are less than squeaky clean. A former head of the Flying Squad added to the succession of errors and misjudgements surrounding the investigation of the April 1993 racist murder of the black teenager Stephen Lawrence. Throughout the subsequent hearing, people in the public gallery were unable to believe their ears and often cried out in shock and disbelief.

Former Detective Chief Superintendent Roderick Barker (ex-head of the Flying Squad) conducted an internal review into the police investigation and concluded that, apart from a few peripheral errors, everything had been properly handled. His report, the Barker Review, formed the basis of the Met's stout defence of its record on this case for four years. Barker was told by the ensuing inquiry's chairman, Sir William McPherson, that his review was 'indefensible'. Sir William added that Barker's testimony to the inquiry, in which he had tried to defend his findings, was 'unreliable', a startling judgement on a man described by one lawyer as the 'crème de la crème' of the Met.

The huge catalogue of errors and inconsistencies in the Stephen Lawrence case are far too many to go into here, but suffice it to say that the Barker Review was a joke. Officers on the scene were given detailed descriptions of the killers by Stephen's friend, Duwayne

Brooks, but failed to act on them; house-to-house enquiries were patchy; a car full of laughing white youths which drove past the scene half an hour after the murder was not tracked down for a week; liaison with the Lawrence family was, in the inquiry chairman's own words, 'hopeless'.

The Dome caper arrived just when the squad was looking for a high-profile success. In addition, it also gave the media-savvy Shatford the chance to join the legendary ranks of Flying Squad 'thief takers' such as Leonard 'Nipper' Read, who ended the Kray twins' reign of terror over London's East End, and Jack Slipper, nemesis of the 1963 Great Train Robbers and a constant thorn in the side of the fugitive Ronnie Biggs. Shatford was also due to retire soon, so capturing the Diamond Geezers would make an appropriate swansong for the detective, almost as much as it would for Terry Millman.

Shatford became operational head of what would become the largest, most expensive Flying Squad operation in history: 'The Flying Squad have done some very big jobs, but in terms of resources and the end results, yes, it was the biggest,' Shatford said. 'About 300 officers were involved, over 100 from the Flying Squad plus firearms and intelligence officers.' He convinced his superiors that such a massive operation was necessary by saying that these were 'serious armed robbers', that 'other criminals walked in fear of them' and that 'they had netted £15 million from financing armed robberies'. While Scotland Yard and subsequently the media accepted Shatford's explanation of the Diamond Geezers' criminal past, a little research suggests that he may have been stretching the truth. For a start, £15 million is an extremely high figure, especially as the total amount of cash stolen in organized heists in the UK as a whole is around £2.5 million each year (according to Metropolitan Police figures). He also said: 'They did one [attempted robbery] before in February 2000 in Nine Elms when they attacked the security van there and escaped across the river, and I was pretty certain then that they took part. I can't prove it, of course, otherwise we would have charged them with it. And then there was another duplicate robbery in Aylesford; again they got away by river there. All my inquiries and investigations said that they did that.'

The Aylesford and Nine Elms robberies would have netted the gang that did the job £8.7 million and £10 million respectively, meaning each member would earn around £1 million (probably half to three-quarters of a million after laundering). According to the Diamond Geezers and police surveillance, they would have netted £500,000 for the Dome job, meaning less than £100,000 each. Instead of a step up from security vans, the theft of the diamonds would actually have been a giant step down in terms of reward.

And it seemed that, according to those who knew them, Betson, Ciarrocchi and Cockran were not part of the security-van or any other robbery attempt, or indeed any serious crime. Did anyone, as Shatford said, 'walk in fear' of Betson, Ciarrocchi and Cockran? 'I know all the serious criminals in London,' said the oldest and most well-connected character who came forward to be interviewed, 'and I can tell you now that none of them would walk in fear of Ray and Bill. No one would; they never gave anyone cause to. They weren't a gang, they didn't even work together. Shatford has to make them look bad because he would look stupid using 300 coppers to catch some lads who were small time.'

Most referred to Cockran as some kind of cuddly animal. One gruff-voiced South Londoner even described him as a 'pussycat'. Another said Cockran was 'totally non-violent', and another that he was 'a teddy bear with not a violent bone in his body'. Cockran may not have paid all of his taxes, but he was not a violent big-time criminal who instilled fear in others. In court it was alleged that Cockran coerced an innocent man to take part in the Dome job. Bringing this up caused much hilarity among those who knew him. 'Bill couldn't coerce an alcoholic into a piss-up,' joked one friend.

Betson was described as 'no angel but a good boy' by one associate and another said: 'I ain't saying he's a saint. He would make his money from cashing forged traveller's cheques.' He was a product of his environment in that crime was a natural career choice, but, again, he was very minor league and certainly never violent.

Not many criminals knew of Ciarrocchi, partly because of his lack of experience: 'Before this [the Dome caper],' said one friend, 'I thought he'd done sod all criminally. I'm surprised to hear he'd been done shoplifting. Lovely boy.'

Essentially, the Diamond Geezers were made up of a core of three petty crooks who were also close friends. Ciarrocchi and Cockran certainly didn't spend their days dreaming of making the 'big score', and the caper came as a complete surprise to each of them when it was suggested by Betson. Betson and Ciarrocchi couldn't pay their bills and needed a lot of cash in a hurry, and Cockran was tempted to join the 'big league', where local heroes were those criminals who would only get out of bed for the 'big scores'. And he always supported his two friends 100 per cent. The fourth Diamond Geezer, Terry Millman, had been a lifelong armed robber but was well past his prime and would not play a major part in the heist itself.

Now, however, they had one more interested party who wanted to ensure that the raid went ahead, but according to a different plan. Nothing was going to go wrong. It would provide the perfect publicity, which would in turn transform the Flying Squad's reputation from that of a corrupt organization to a much-loved Sweeney for the new millennium. And what name did Shatford give to the operation?

He called it Operation Magician.

7 – THE WEAKEST LINKS

'Make sure your wheelman's a diamond.'

EX-GETAWAY DRIVER, MICKEY 'THE LIP' AGUDA

With such a big job, simple though it seemed to Betson and Cockran, there were always going to be problems. Much to Betson's exasperation, the amateurish behaviour of some members of the Diamond Geezers occasionally put the whole job at risk.

Terry Millman had been in charge of collecting the necessary vehicles for the job and had managed to get hold of the speedboat for £2,000, paid for in cash (Millman, with his typical humour, signed the receipt 'Terry Diamond'). The JCB had already been supplied by a criminal contact, but by mid-September 2000, two untraceable Transit vans were still needed. So one cold, damp night in Clapton, Millman popped out to see if he could pinch them.

Millman first tried to open a van door with a twisted coat hanger but it slipped from his hands and clattered to the ground. In the damp it was difficult to hold, even more so if you were a little the worse for drink. Also, Millman found that he was in so much pain from the cancer now that when he tried to bend down and pick it up he had to stop. He then collected a loose brick from a skip and chucked it through the Transit's window. No alarm went off.

Millman climbed in, not before smashing out the remaining glass, so that no sign of the broken window remained.

Despite the freezing night air, Millman was sweating from his effort, pain and fever by the time the engine turned over and finally chugged into life. He was feeling pretty poorly; the cancer had him in its death grip. It didn't help that he was being blasted with fresh air thanks to the smashed window. Desperate for something warming, he fumbled in his inside jacket pocket and produced a flask of rum as the van lurched around the Minories in the City of London's financial district. He took a swig, and as he did so he jerked the wheel, causing the van to veer off at a sharp angle, and as he turned into the approach road to cross Tower Bridge he struck the back of a parked black cab.

Millman was relieved to discover that he was relatively unharmed, if a little shaken up and dizzy. But things were about to get even worse. A police car flicked its siren on and off to let Millman know that they were on the scene, but, by the time they had pulled up, Millman's criminal instincts had already told him to run. Despite his weakness, the adrenalin had kicked in and he had vanished around the corner before the policemen were out of their car. His escape was fortunate, bordering on the miraculous. Eventually, Millman managed to steal two Transit vans in another part of East London.

Aldo Ciarrocchi had also been sailing close to the wind. One evening a few days earlier, in a housing estate a stone's throw from the Walworth Road, Ciarrocchi was also looking around to see if anyone was watching him. He was in a car park which was sheltered by three tower blocks. He gave the place one more look round before taking a small oblong device from inside his coat pocket. He crouched down and placed the smoke grenade carefully on the ground, pulled the pin and ran back a few paces. Ciarrocchi wanted to check that the smoke grenades they were planning to use were up to the job. He counted to five and then stood back, expecting something to happen, but nothing did. He took two steps forwards before the smoke grenade suddenly made a pop and started to spurt out a little smoke. Disappointed, Ciarrocchi thought that he was going to have to go and have words with the supplier, but the smoke suddenly began to get thicker and thicker and eventually started pouring out at quite a rate. In a couple of minutes smoke filled the car park, obscuring everything. By now people were leaning out of windows, terrified that their high-rise flats were on fire. Women started screaming for their children and people poured out of the flats. As the sirens from the fire brigade approached, Ciarrocchi took to his heels and fled.

Finally, on the morning of 6 October 2000, the Diamond Geezers were ready. But so was the Flying Squad, thanks mainly to the efforts of the specialist surveillance unit. By establishing that the Diamond Geezers needed to use a boat and therefore needed the highest possible tide at the Dome, they were able to predict on which days the raid would be most likely to take place. On those days, the police would stake out the Dome in readiness – they could never be certain, though, whether the raid would go ahead or not. But this time, reports from the observation teams at Tong Farm and Old Coal Yard in Plumstead, the Diamond Geezers' London base for their vehicles, had made it clear to Shatford that there had been increased activity over the past few days, suggesting that 6 October, the day of the highest tide in Greenwich that month, would be the best time for the Diamond Geezers to strike.

At 3 a.m., Detective Superintendent Jon Shatford briefed 200 police officers from Operation Magician's on-site headquarters, the Dome's CCTV room, Bronze Control. Shatford reminded the officers (mistakenly) that this gang of ruthless, ambitious armed robbers would be carrying guns. He told them to be aware that innocent Dome workers could be near by when the order was given to arrest the suspects and that their safety was paramount. Shatford said afterwards: 'My biggest nightmare was that a member of the public would be seriously injured.'

Among those policemen present were forty specialist firearms officers from SO19. Some of these were hidden behind a secret wall within the Dome. Others were sent into the Dome in disguise. Dressed as cleaners, they concealed their guns in black plastic bags and rubbish bins. Surveillance officers disguised as Dome employees also patrolled the area.

A further sixty armed Flying Squad officers were stationed around the Thames, and twenty were in boats on the river itself. Officers were also positioned at a number of observation points between the Old Coal Yard in Plumstead and the Dome. Shatford said: 'It is still thankfully unusual to arm in those numbers.' But when asked if they were ready to 'take them out', he answered in the affirmative without a moment's hesitation. 'If even fake guns were raised against any of my officers who were armed, I would have no criticism of them whatsoever if they were to shoot the person holding them.' Two police helicopters and several specialist police pursuit drivers were also on standby in case anyone escaped. A criminal gang had not been so outnumbered since Butch Cassidy and the Sundance Kid had taken on the entire Bolivian army. 'My whole strategy was to arrest them with overwhelming force,' said Shatford, 'to totally overpower them and make it clear to them from the outset that there was no chance of escape or resistance.' There had previously been days when Shatford thought the Diamond Geezers were about to strike, but was unable to provide overwhelming force. On those occasions Shatford ordered the vault closed.

Also present on that morning were dozens of forensic officers who were briefed separately by Shatford and his deputy, Detective Inspector Swinfield. Their role would also be crucial: collecting evidence from the JCB and its contents to every last fibre that could be found in the vicinity of the vault.

Around 200 officers, 100 armed, were lying in wait for the Diamond Geezers like coiled springs. They didn't know what to expect. They had been told that the gang would be armed, that they were ruthless. They didn't know from which direction they were coming or exactly what their plan was to get the diamonds out of the vault and escape. Their lives could be in danger.

Also in attendance was the new executive chairman of the Dome, the charismatic, plain-speaking sixty-five-year-old David James, who had been told about the raid just two days after he started work at the beleaguered Dome on 8 September. 'We were David James's worst nightmare,' said Shatford. 'What with everything else at the Dome, to be presented with the fact that there was going to be an armed robbery, well, his reaction was one of incredulity, and I had to do some strong talking to convince him.'

Mr James said: 'I didn't believe it at first. My first instinct was to prevent the raid. I then approached someone in the Cabinet who said I should assist the police as far as possible but that the ultimate responsibility for safety rested on me as accounting officer.' Mr James and the French chief executive, Pierre-Yves Gerbeau, who had been brought over from Disneyland Europe to rescue the Dome, were the only two civilians who knew about the possible heist and had the unfortunate duty of taking it in turns to show up for work at 3 a.m. on the days when the police thought that the raid might happen. Shatford was also not exactly flavour of the month with the owner of the Millennium Collection, De Beers' chairman, Nicky Oppenheimer. Oppenheimer was trying to get over the death of his father Harry on 19 August 2000 and administer his complex £2.5 billion estate when Shatford broke the news.

On the morning of 6 October, the minutes dragged inexorably as London's street lights gradually surrendered to the grey autumnal daylight. Those officers waiting on the Thames shivered and stretched in their boats. The Dome slowly began to come to life as people arrived for work and headed for breakfast at the on-site canteen, a hundred yards from the diamond vault. Officers' bellies rumbled as the smell of coffee and bacon wafted through the massive structure. The atmosphere among the officers was calm, but as time dragged on the tension inevitably grew.

Shatford watched anxiously from Bronze Control as the man in charge of the CCTV, Detective Constable Allen, tested and checked the cameras that would trace the Diamond Geezers' approach. Unfortunately, these cameras could not help officers inside the Dome, who had no idea where the vehicle was coming from or exactly what was going to happen. Shatford, fearing that the Diamond Geezers had sophisticated listening equipment, had instructed that all officers should maintain a strict radio silence so they could not be alerted.

Shatford was at this point under intense pressure. Responsibility for any mistake, despite Dome chairman David James's assurance that he was in fact ultimately responsible, would be Shatford's to bear. Shatford had chosen to make sure that this attempted heist took place so that the Flying Squad would be ready to catch the gang red-handed. 'If they'd been alerted to our presence anywhere, from Tong Farm to the Dome, they would have simply vanished and we'd have no way of finding out where they'd vanished to,' Shatford explained. 'Then they'd plan an equally audacious or dangerous robbery, be it a bank, post office or wherever, and then there was the danger that a cashier or security guard would get killed, that was my fear. So I had to balance the fact that I was pretty sure that they were going to rob the Dome, so if I could control that and gather enough evidence and do it in a secure enough way to prevent anyone being harmed, then I would prevent any further risk of them harming anyone else. There was risk to it, but to me the greater risk was to let them get away and then commit a crime where there are no mechanisms in place to mitigate the risk.' Now all he could do was wait and hope that when he gave the order to arrest the Diamond Geezers, the overwhelming force would lead to a quick surrender.

Finally, as the zones were being switched into life by their attendants, the Diamond Geezers were spotted leaving Old Coal Yard. They were in a three-vehicle convoy consisting of the two vans stolen by Millman and the JCB. Officers posted along the route watched keenly as the convoy separated. Millman drove Hurley to the pick-up point north of the Thames, while the JCB with Betson at the wheel trundled steadily along towards the target. The van with Cockran, Tony and Ciarrocchi, who was monitoring police transmissions, followed Betson. They were all being recorded by surveillance cameras.

Those in the second van joked nervously among themselves, trying to steady their nerves as they approached their target, the subject of many months' planning. Betson's resolve was absolute. It had to be now, he told himself; he had to get the job done, for his friends and family who were counting on him. Betson had brought his friends on the raid, and it was his responsibility to get them out as free and wealthy men. Betson confirmed via walkie-talkie that Millman and Hurley were at the launch point for the boat.

A horrified Cockran was the first to notice that they were being followed by a police car. Cockran's horror was easily matched by Shatford's as this was most definitely not part of his plan. To nab the Diamond Geezers prior to the raid would not do. The police would only be able to prosecute them for the minor offence of 'going equipped' for robbery. Shatford could only pray that the car didn't pull over the JCB or van, which would mean the end of Operation Magician. Meanwhile, Ciarrocchi made doubly sure that they were not the subject of a conversation on police radio. As far as he could tell, no one was listening in. Meanwhile, Betson looked anxiously in his mirror and could just see the police car behind the van being driven by Cockran. Betson was afraid that if the police car overtook him, then they might spot his latex mask.

Then Betson got a call from Millman alerting him to the fact that the boat wasn't starting. After an anxious two minutes while Hurley and Millman tried to figure out what was wrong, Betson made the decision to abort. The van and JCB were watched by observation teams turning at a roundabout and heading back to Old Coal Yard. The police car drove on, unaware of the panic it had caused in criminals and police alike.

Gradually, Shatford realized with a sinking heart that the raid was not going to happen that day. 'To go through all that careful preparation, the effort of smuggling officers into the Dome, for them to have to hang around in disguise, or behind walls, even in rubbish bins, for six hours plus, and all for nothing was a real blow. It was just incredibly frustrating.'

As well as Betson, Shatford was now feeling the pressure. Being in charge of this massive operation was a great strain, professionally and personally. He was expected to succeed by his superiors. There was no room for error. An exhausted Shatford was on the job practically twenty-four hours a day. Scotland Yard would frown heavily on the Flying Squad's most expensive operation going pear-shaped. The fact that he could be accused of wasting money on a massive and expensive surveillance operation was not sitting comfortably with him. The Flying Squad detectives had other operations to attend to, and so were also suffering the extra pressure brought about by Operation Magician, and among some of them Shatford was not exactly their favourite person. The conditions for surveillance were less than perfect, as Shatford admitted: 'It was the wettest summer ever that year. We had surveillance people living up trees and in flooded ditches, and equipment was damaged. We had significant difficulties to overcome.'

Betson's decision to abort might well have meant the end of Operation Magician because if there were inside men – bent security guards, for example – then they may well have realized by now that the police were on to them and word would have got back to the Diamond Geezers. Perhaps inside men had spotted the police presence in the Dome and told the gang to abort. It was a testing time for the Flying Squad.

This was by no means the end of the operational problems for the Diamond Geezers either. 'The tides wouldn't be right for a while, and in the end we decided that we'd try again on 6 November,' said Betson. Then the week before, the Diamond Geezers lost their boatman.

Hurley had suddenly got cold feet. There were good reasons for this. He was not in such urgent need of finances as the others. He had successfully dealt in property and had a paid-for villa and a heavily pregnant girlfriend waiting for him in Marbella. As the tides meant that they would have to wait another month before they could try again, there was a chance he would miss the birth. And, of course, if they were caught, it would mean that he would miss the early life of his first child.

Betson did his best to persuade Hurley to stay in, but it was no good. Hurley's mind was made up. He was concerned that after all this time spent preparing, the police would find out what they were up to. In his opinion there were too many variables; they had tried, but they had missed their opportunity. On 31 October 2000, after promises over drinks that they would soon see each other again, but in Marbella, Hurley headed for the airport. Betson, envious that Hurley could afford to make that kind of decision, determinedly turned back to the job in hand. His natural stubbornness was not going to let Hurley's trepidation put him off committing the crime of the millennium. As leader of the Diamond Geezers, he felt he had a responsibility to his partners in crime as well as to his family. But the gang needed a replacement, and fast. Any further delay and the cash-strapped Diamond Geezers would have to wait until December before the tide would be right again. With this in mind, Cockran drove down to Brighton to call in an urgent favour.

Thirty-four-year-old Kevin Meredith ran (and still does today) a fishing boat called the *Random Harvest* from Brighton Marina and, for a fee, will take people out for a day's fishing. Cockran met Meredith in 1998, after a friend recommended him and he hired his boat to do just that. Meredith grew up in Brighton and was a pupil at Longhill School, Rottingdean. His father, Les Meredith, always had boats, and the young Meredith went into the charter-boat business when he left school at sixteen. Meredith is a small, wiry man. He has quite a weather-beaten appearance and has a fiercely devoted wife, who didn't like him spending time away from home. In fact, if Meredith's wife had insisted, then he might have rejected Bill Cockran's advances, but, according to Meredith, Cockran had some pretty persuasive reasons for him to come to London to help the Diamond Geezers out.

'Bill had been out fishing on the boat in Brighton a couple of times,' said Meredith. 'We got on quite well, and on his second trip I told him about my problems with the boat and that the moorings [rent on the harbour space] were due. Six customers had failed to turn up on that day, and I was counting on their money to help pay the moorings, so I was fuming about that. I told him that this happened all the time.'

Meredith said that he was shocked when Cockran offered him the money. He said he had not asked for a loan and was surprised at the offer: 'He said he would lend me the money, but you know what people are like. I didn't think he would actually do it, but he did. I received £1,400 about a week later. Bill said it was interest-free. I used it to pay £1,000 due on the moorings and between £250 and £300 on telephone bills.'

Mike Snelling, a sixty-year-old retired maritime pilot who runs the 43-foot *Girl Gray* charter vessel at the Marina, has known Meredith for twenty years and is full of praise for his fellow boatman: 'He's a pleasant lad, very sociable, cheerful and helpful. He likes a joke and is always pleasant. We were all taken by surprise when this happened and Kevin's name came up. I reckon he was drawn in to all this by villains.' Indeed, Meredith argues that he was forced to take part in the raid on the Dome. He makes a point of saying that the only crime he had committed previously was to fail to pay his TV licence, for which he was successfully prosecuted.

Meredith said: 'Bill [Cockran] called on Saturday 4 November and asked if I wanted a drink, a cup of coffee. I agreed to meet him, and he asked me: "Have you got the [loan] money?" I said: "No, I haven't." He then asked me if I could captain a speedboat. Surprised, I replied: "I've never driven a speedboat."

'Bill then said: "I ain't got a lot of time on it. I need to know. If you can, then I want you to come back with me to London tomorrow." I was reluctant. I told him that he'd put me in a bit of a situation. Bill then told me: "Remember your wife and kids." And so I gave a hesitant yes. At first I thought it was perfectly honest and would be very good money. It was odd. It didn't cross my mind at first that it was criminal. At that stage, I had no inclination [*sic*] that anything odd was up.' When asked what he understood about the reference to his wife and kids, he answered: 'Well, I wasn't too sure. I knew he was a bit of a wide boy, you know, and I thought if I said no, what's going to happen? I started to think this is way out of my league. I lied to my wife. I wasn't going to tell her that somebody had threatened her and the kids.' Meredith's wife noticed that he was very quiet when he came home that Saturday evening. Meredith then upset her by saying that he was 'going off building in London' as an excuse.

As may be expected, Cockran tells a rather different story: 'I picked Kevin because I know he knows about boats. I had rung his father to make an appointment at 4 p.m. on Saturday 4 November, and we arranged to meet in a busy pub. I did not mention the debt at the public house, definitely not. I had said on the phone: "You're in for a drink and forget about the money." He would know that the meeting was not to collect the debt.

'I did not say anything about the diamonds, as I thought it right not to tell him, but he knew that we were up to something. I offered him a drink and told him he would have a nice holiday out of it. I suggested he would make an easy £10,000.'

Meredith denies this: 'I never heard him say anything about a holiday for my wife and kids, and there was no mention of money. He said: "Remember your wife and kids." But it was the way he looked at me, his eyes, which made me think it was a threat.'

Cockran said: 'I would never threaten a guy's wife and children ... possibly he may have misunderstood. All I said was about going on holiday with the wife and children ... I would not have thought that Meredith was frightened of me. He might make up stories to save his own skin.'

Despite the 'misunderstanding', Meredith agreed: 'I met Bill the next day in the car park at the [Brighton] ice rink. He said that somebody had dropped out of the job, leaving a vacancy. I don't know why, but I didn't ask him what he was talking about. I took my car and followed him to London in his van, and he sorted me out a place to stay on the Sunday night.'

Then he met Betson: 'I took Meredith to the top floor of some council flats,' said Betson, 'and there we could see *A Slice of Reality*. I showed him the beach and told him that was the place to collect us from.'

On the morning of 6 November, the second attempt on the Dome swung into action.

'On Monday morning,' said Meredith, 'we left the flat. Millman and the other blokes all got into a van together, and I was offered ammonia by Tony. He showed it to me and said, "This is a weak solution of ammonia," to which I said, "No." Cockran began to explain that "It's obviously only for..." but Tony then started talking about radios. I didn't want to know what it was for. I was feeling scared. I didn't feel that I could get out of what was going on.' According to Betson, the ammonia, contained in small vials of Vic nasal spray, was to be used to contaminate any DNA evidence (blood, sweat, hair) that they might leave behind on the vehicles, in the vault and on the glass.

This time, the raid got off to a smoother start. Shatford had again briefed the detectives at 3 a.m. and spent the morning drinking coffee and watching everything on the CCTV in Bronze Control. Again, the adrenalin was pumping. Shatford said: 'I knew it was going to happen because I stood up and started to pace. We were in a high state of alert.' Shatford's apprehension grew as he watched his targets get closer and closer to their target. Two hundred officers, the cars, the boats, the helicopters and forensic teams were all in position, and surreptitious efforts were being made to keep people away from the vault area. You could almost smell the testosterone.

The JCB was nearing the Dome when it suddenly stopped. Everybody who could see (the officers in the Dome didn't know what was going on yet as they had been told to keep radio silence) held their breath. The JCB reversed, did a three-point turn and headed back to Old Coal Yard. An exasperated Shatford had to report to his superiors that the attempt had been postponed for unknown reasons yet again. The question on all the officers' lips was 'why?' and Shatford said: 'We wondered if we had been rumbled.' But if they'd checked their tides table, then they would have had the answer.

The heist had been cancelled by Meredith: 'I called the job off because the tide was wrong ... the highest tide would actually be the next day, on 7 November. I was devastated. I rang my wife. She thought I was with another woman.'

8 – LATE ADDITION

'He's a bit of a quiet one is Bob. Doesn't say much, but what he does say counts.'

BILL COCKRAN ON ROBERT 'BOB THE BUILDER' ADAMS

Remarkably, on the night of 6 November 2000, Betson recruited one more member into the prestigious club that was the Diamond Geezers, fifty-five-year-old Robert Adams. Born in Islington, North London, the former plasterer was nicknamed 'Bob the Builder' and had known Betson for several years. Adams was tall, tanned and muscular, with a bulbous nose and a hard, deep-wrinkled face. A man of few words, he had little to say to anyone apart from the occasional quip or observation. Verbally, he couldn't have been more different from Millman, who was chatty and witty.

It wasn't clear what Betson thought that the ex-plasterer would bring to the Diamond Geezers, but the police had a theory. A police spokesperson later told the press that Adams had a previous conviction and was sentenced to six years for attempting to kill his wife. The ex-commander of the Flying Squad, John O'Connor, said: 'Most jobs, you want one or two psychopaths involved.' Psychopaths are focused on self-preservation and success and have few moral qualms about violence. They would see a 'job' through to the end and ask no questions. According to the police, Adams was that psychopath.

Shatford said: 'What he also had was credibility among criminals as being reliable and someone not to be messed with, someone who could be trusted.' Shatford added that he was a member of the infamous North London crime family, the Adamses. The Adamses are one of London's most powerful and most lunatic crime families. They took part in an infamous gun battle on the leafy streets of Islington (once home to a pre-Prime Minister Tony Blair and family) with their bitter rivals, the Reillys.

The Reilly and the Adams crime families had a long history of hating each other. This particular incident started on New Year's Day 1990, when Georgie Reilly, an armed robber, was insulted in front of his wife by one of the Adamses' henchmen. Reilly ran home, dropped off his wife, armed himself with a gun and went looking for 'satisfaction'. The Adamses got to hear of this, and as result Pat Adams strolled into the Prince Alfred pub, owned by the Reillys, knowing full well that this would incite righteous indignation.

Soon a red BMW full of armed Reillys pulled in to Huntingdon Street ready to 'take him out'. Patsy, however, was not alone. Concealed at a junction close to the pub were two carloads of armed and drug-fuelled Adamses. A few seconds later it was like a scene out of the film *Heat*, and residents had to run for their lives as bullets bounced off walls, pavements, cars and roads. The bullet-ridden BMW reversed, guns still being fired through the windows, as it performed a U-turn and sped off, taking the battle to the heart of the City of London, the capital's financial district.

Although these were two of London's most successful crime families, they were not very good shots. No one was hurt. The only person to be jailed was nightclub owner Jonny Reilly, who received a fairly minor sentence of thirty months for violent conduct after the police managed to find the red BMW and link it to him.

The Adams family, based in Islington but with bases in Spain and elsewhere, are believed to have assets worth over £50 million. They once made an ambitious attempt to take over Arsenal football club and have attracted the attention of MI5. They have since moved operations to Spain (Pat Adams has a house there) but still manage to dominate the British drugs trade, in particular the dealing of ecstasy in nightclubs.

Looking at the pedigree of the Adams family, it would be easy to accept that Bob Adams was the 'gang psycho'. But this was far from the truth. Adams was called 'Bob the Builder' because he was a plasterer by trade. He had no criminal record until quite recently. He worked, was married, had a house and was doing very well for himself. He was offered a lucrative eighteen-month contract to work in Saudi Arabia. While he was there, he lived the quiet life and sent most of his money home to his wife, whom he would visit only occasionally. Eventually, the contract was up and he flew home. He took a taxi from the airport, walked up to the door, and as he was about to insert his key his best friend opened it. Adams was very happy to see his friend and then asked him where his wife was.

But his friend said: 'Go away, Bob. You don't live here no more.' Adams didn't quite grasp what he was being told at first, but his friend explained the situation to him as bluntly as possible: 'I live here now, with your wife, you don't. Now go away.' Adams refused to budge and stood his ground, until his 'friend' pulled out a kitchen knife and said: 'Leave, or I'll have to use this.'

At this Adams turned and walked back down the garden path towards the cab that was still parked in the road. Surprised that Adams had given up so readily, his friend started to shut the front door. But as he did so, Adams spun around suddenly, ran at the door, kicked it open and jumped on him. His wife, who'd been watching from the top of the stairs, screamed and ran downstairs as the two men struggled on the floor for control of the jagged knife, which was pushed back and forth between the two men, at one point cutting Adams on the face. Then, suddenly, the struggle stopped and there was an agonized bellow from Adams's ex-friend and another scream from his wife. The knife was protruding from the man's stomach.

Still seeing red, Adams belted his wife across the face with the back of his hand and walked out of the house and into the street. After pacing the streets aimlessly for a few hours, he turned himself in at the local police station. He was arrested and tried for the attempted murder of the 'friend'. Thankfully, the victim was not seriously injured from the knife wound, but Adams was none the less sentenced to six years in prison.

Prior to this, Adams had had a clean record. But while in prison he made friends. Adams had nothing left on the outside now: no family to speak of, no business, no work, nothing but some new friends who had promised to help him out when he was released. He took them up on the offer and for a while he did a bit of minor-league cannabis dealing. As word got around the South-East London criminal community that Adams was a plasterer, he was offered some lucrative cash jobs to plaster the homes of the criminal *nouveau riche* in Kent. This is how he got to know Cockran and, through Cockran, Betson.

According to members of the infamous crime family of the same name, Bob Adams was not a relation. He was not a psychopath. He had fallen into the life of a petty criminal but was a complete amateur. Betson said he approached Adams because he could be trusted to do a good job and 'needed a break'.

'After his wife left him and he got out of jail, Adams was a lonely character, living alone, watching the telly while eating a TV dinner, that sort of thing,' said Betson. 'He was a good man, though, a reliable skilled worker, but he was skint, living in a rented bedsit, and he was tired, old and tired.'

Adams should have been looking forward to a comfortable and lengthy retirement on a fat pension with a second home abroad, but instead he was going to spend his old age in poverty. The idea to bring Adams in was suggested by Cockran, who argued that it would be better for Betson to wait in the JCB, keeping the engine running and saving vital seconds. Someone else could help Cockran smash the glass and cut the diamonds out of the display. He certainly couldn't manage it on his own. Cockran and Betson decided that they should ask Adams and give him the job of smashing the weakened glass with a sledgehammer.

Cockran visited Adams in his flat in Bermondsey on the evening of 6 November. 'He sat there quietly. He'd just finished a plastering job and was having a beer in front of the telly with dried plaster in his hair. I told him that this was a once-in-a-lifetime chance to make himself enough money to retire comfortably on.

'He thought I was joking at first,' said Cockran. 'Then, when he realized that I was serious, he just looked off into the distance and didn't say a word. He's a bit of a quiet one is Bob. Doesn't say much, but what he does say counts. I asked him if he was in or out and that I needed a decision right now, this minute. Bob stayed silent, and I was on my way out, thinking he meant no, when he suddenly stood up. I saw the look in his eye, and from that I already knew he was up for it. He said: "Fuck it. I'm in."'

The Diamond Geezers were finally ready to go to work.

9 – FOR WHAT IT'S WORTH

'It's a priceless diamond as long as he doesn't try to sell it.'

DIAMOND-MINE OWNER, ALBERT JOLIS

Meanwhile, at the heart of all this intense build-up and activity sat the De Beers Millennium Collection. The Millennium Star itself, at 203.04 carats, is arguably the world's most perfect pear-shaped diamond. Its eleven satellites, also exceptional in their own right, are each worth a fortune. The Heart of Eternity is rated as one of the most beautiful diamonds in the world. In fact the 27.64-carat, heart-shaped stone, which sparkles in an intense blue, is considered by some diamond experts to be more remarkable than the Star.

But what exactly was the collection worth? Some, particularly those in the diamond trade, may dispute the estimates of the diamonds' worth as published in the press (£150 to £350 million). The Millennium Collection is without doubt a very rare set of diamonds. But the Diamond Geezers may have been surprised to know that just a few miles north of Greenwich, at the Diamond Trading Company's headquarters at 2 Charterhouse Street, four billion diamonds sit in De Beers' vaults.

Four *billion* diamonds. Diamonds are not as rare as we are led to believe. They were pretty hard to come by until mining practices became super-efficient. In addition, thanks to improving skills and technology throughout the twentieth century, dozens of profitable diamond mines have been discovered in the world, from Siberia to Australia and, most recently, Canada. The only reason diamonds are so expensive is because De Beers have orchestrated a practice whereby they purchase most of the diamonds produced directly from mines and keep them behind locked doors, releasing only a limited number to keep the market price buoyant. De Beers' former chairman, Ernest Oppenheimer, said as far back as 1910: 'Common sense tells us that the only way to increase the value of diamonds is to make them scarce – that is, to reduce the production.'

The other way to ensure that diamonds are still seen as precious and worth paying several thousand pounds for is through marketing, something that De Beers have been extremely successful at doing. De Beers have produced some of the most intelligent marketing in advertising history. In 1929 the Oppenheimer family, owners of the Anglo-American Corporation, seized control of De Beers. It was a critical time because America was entering the Depression and diamond prices were sinking. De Beers' new owners hired the N. W. Ayer advertising agency to transform the public imagination about the diamond. To do that, the company hired psychologists to burrow into American buying habits. And it hired the most visionary artists in the world to help. At the office of N. W. Ayer in New York City, there hangs original art produced by Picasso, Salvador Dali and others for the De Beers account.

De Beers made movies to show diamonds being given as engagement rings; the larger the ring, the greater the love shown by the man and the higher status the woman would achieve in society. They even used the British royal family. N. W. Ayer's advertising proposal to De Beers read: 'Since Great Britain has such an important interest in the diamond industry, the royal couple could be of tremendous assistance to this British industry by wearing diamonds rather than other jewels.' Queen Elizabeth was presented with a commemorative diamond by Harry Oppenheimer when she visited De Beers' South African diamond mines.

During the Second World War, N. W. Ayer fed numerous stories to the press suggesting that the diamond market would not be affected by the conflict. The war did in fact shut down pretty much all the mines, and production was almost at a standstill in Africa. Despite this, the headlines kept on coming: 'Diamond, King of Gems, Reigns Supreme Despite War', 'Diamond Supply Unhurt by War', 'War Gives Impetus to Diamond Cutting', 'Marriage Increases Indicated by Rise in Diamond Sales', and 'How Diamonds Spark the Wings of War and Peace'.

In three years, diamond sales rocketed by 55 per cent. The campaign gathered pace as people were told in advertisements and newspaper articles that buying diamonds would help the war effort and was a patriotic thing to do. Lecturers visited high schools and impressed on young minds the virtue of owning a diamond ring. Portraits were commissioned of engaged socialites flashing massive diamond rings in the lens of the photographer.

Then in 1948 came a real breakthrough in De Beers' advertising. Late one night in 1947, at the New York offices of N. W. Ayer and Son Advertising, copywriter Frances Gerety was putting the finishing touches on a De Beers campaign when she realized she had forgotten to include a signature line. When interviewed many years later about her role in the development of what has come to be one of the world's definitive statements about diamonds, Ms Gerety recounted that, feeling exhausted, she put her head down and said: 'Please, God, send me a line.' She then scribbled 'A Diamond Is Forever'. A year later her words were the official logo of De Beers. In 2000 those famous four words were voted top advertising slogan of the century by the prestigious US magazine *Advertising Age*, beating Nike ('Just Do It'), Coca-Cola ('The Pause That Refreshes'), Avis ('We Try Harder') and a host of others. De Beers marketing director for the USA, Mary Walsh, said: 'It is so simple and yet so profound and, although it's been around for a long time, it's as fresh and appropriate for the coming millennium diamond-buying opportunities as if it had been written yesterday.' Sadly, Ms Gerety didn't make it to see her slogan go on beyond the millennium. She passed away in April 1999 at the age of eighty-three. She never married.

Ironically, diamonds are not forever. They can be chipped, shattered, discoloured or heated until they turn to ash. The slogan, however, helped De Beers to persuade owners that they should never sell their diamonds, even in times of economic hardship, because they were a gift of everlasting love.

The advertising campaigns helped De Beers to expand their sales in the United States from a mere $23 million in 1939 to over $2 billion at the wholesale level by 1980. This was remarkable, but not nearly as incredible as De Beers' achievement in Japan, where until the mid-1960s Japanese parents arranged marriages for their children and the ceremony was marked by the bride and groom both drinking rice wine from the same wooden bowl. This simple arrangement had persisted for more than a millennium. Then, in 1967, De Beers decided to change the Japanese courtship ritual. The advertising agency began its campaign by subtly suggesting that diamonds were a visible sign of modern Western values. The message in these ads was clear: diamonds represent a sharp break with the Oriental past and an entry point into modern life. Until 1959 the importation of diamonds had not even been permitted by the post-war Japanese government. When the campaign began in 1968, less than 5 per cent of Japanese women getting married received a diamond engagement ring. By 1981, some 60 per cent of Japanese brides wore diamonds. In a mere thirteen years, the fifteen-hundred-year Japanese tradition was radically revised. Diamonds became a staple of the Japanese marriage. Japan became, after the United States, the second-largest market for the sale of diamond engagement rings.

The true genius of De Beers lies in creating and sustaining in the popular imagination a connection between something that has no value at all and something that is extremely valuable, which is human love. You can't eat a diamond, you can't drive it home, you can't make clothes out of it, you can't build houses out of it, yet it has come to be seen to possess a priceless symbolic importance. Perhaps the greatest irony of this story is that two of the protagonists in the Dome robbery, Betson and Ciarrocchi, are examples of that connection: two men, each in love, each wanting to commit to making a new life with their partners, but for them this meant taking diamonds rather than giving them.

Most knowledgeable diamond dealers believe that the value of extraordinarily large diamonds, such as the Millennium Star or the 'Taylor–Burton Diamond', bought and sold by Elizabeth Taylor, depends more on cunning publicity than the intrinsic quality of the stone. An extreme example of this is the 70-carat diamond given to Emperor Bokassa in 1977 by Albert Jolis, president of Diamond Distributors Inc. The Jolis family first negotiated a concession to mine diamonds in 1947 in what was then the French colony of Ubangi in Africa.

In 1966 Bokassa, a colonel, seized power in a military coup and proclaimed himself president of what now became the Central African Republic. President Bokassa agreed to continue the Jolis concession in return for the government receiving a share of the profit. A decade later, however, when Bokassa decided to become emperor and re-christened the country the 'Central African Empire', Jolis was given to understand that he was expected to provide a 'very large diamond' for the coronation.

As the coronation date approached, Jolis found himself caught in a difficult situation. His firm could not afford to spend millions of dollars to acquire the sort of diamond that would put the emperor-to-be in a league with the Shah of Iran or the British royal family; yet if he presented him with a small diamond, Bokassa might well withdraw his firm's diamond concessions.

Finally, Jolis hit on a possible solution to this dilemma. One of his assistants had found a large chunk of industrial diamond boart, weighing nearly 70 carats, which curiously resembled Africa in shape. This piece of black, poorly crystallized diamond would ordinarily have been crushed into abrasive powder, and as such would have been worth about $2 a carat, or $140 (£92). Jolis instead ordered that this large diamond be polished and mounted on a large ring. He then had one of his workmen set a quarter-carat white diamond at the point in the black stone that would coincide with the location of the capital of the Central African Empire. Finally, Jolis placed the ring in a presentation box with a certificate stating that this diamond, which resembled the continent of Africa, was unique in all the world.

The following week, understandably nervous about how it would be received by Bokassa, Jolis flew to the Central African Republic capital, Bangui, and presented the ring. Bokassa took it out of the box, examined it carefully for a moment, then took Jolis by the hand and led him into a room where his entire Cabinet was assembled. He paraded around the table, jubilantly displaying to each and every one of his ministers this huge black diamond. A few days later, the Emperor proudly wore the black diamond during the coronation ceremony. The world press reported that this 70-carat diamond, which had cost Jolis less than $500, was worth over $500,000 (£274,000). A piece of industrial boart was thus elevated to being one of the most celebrated crown jewels in the world.

The Bokassa empire ended in 1979 when French paratroopers, on orders from Paris, staged a bloodless coup and put the Emperor and his retinue on a jet headed for France. From there, Bokassa went into exile on the Ivory Coast with his prize diamond ring. When Jolis heard that Bokassa retained among his crown jewels the industrial diamond Jolis had presented to him two years earlier, he commented: 'It's a priceless diamond as long as he doesn't try to sell it.'

The value of the Emperor's diamond, like that of most other diamonds, therefore depends heavily on the perception of the buyer. If it is accepted as a unique gem and a crown jewel, it could be auctioned off for £1 million. If, on the other hand, it is seen as a piece of industrial boart, it will be sold for £100 and used as grinding powder. The diamond trade is, as Jolis observed, 'a two-tier market'.

So who on earth would buy the Millennium Star, with its inestimable price tag from De Beers? Well, funnily enough, the answer is De Beers. De Beers LV to be precise, the retail arm of the Diamond Trading Company. Until 2001 De Beers had steered clear of the retail side of the business but finally decided to launch a joint venture with luxury-goods maker Louis Vuitton of London's Bond

Street in December 2001. Part of the reason for this was to try to break into the American market as direct operations are forbidden in America, its biggest market, because the De Beers cartel breaks antitrust rules. In 1994 the Department of Justice charged De Beers in a price-fixing scheme. The company failed to turn up in court, which is why you'll never see a De Beers executive enjoying a champagne breakfast at Tiffany's on Fifth Avenue, or anywhere else in the United States. But by forming a new company officially independent of the De Beers Diamond Trading Company and by sharing operations with LVMH, the luxury-goods group that owns Louis Vuitton, De Beers may soon be able to open luxury shops in the United States and promote its sparkling wares in this way. The highlight of the opening ceremony was the display of their invaluable asset, the Millennium Star, worn on a necklace by model Heidi Merril (Alain Lorenzo, chief executive of De Beers LV, would like to make it clear that the Millennium Star is most definitely not kept at the store).

As De Beers LV are officially independent, they have to buy their stock from De Beers, and this rule applied to the Millennium Star. De Beers are reluctant to say how exactly this strange purchase was handled and at what cost, but a Companies House search of De Beers LV reveals that their total investment in stock in 2001 was approximately £26 million.

So what was the value of the Millennium Star? To De Beers it was priceless because of the publicity that went with it. It had to be believed to be priceless for the marketing to work. To the public, the diamond would be the equivalent of the *Mona Lisa*, something that could be admired in a museum but would never look right on a mantelpiece. To the thieves, the diamonds were worth a few hundred thousand pounds at the most. This is what they expected to be paid for them. What would they be worth to the person who bought them? Other than De Beers, who would want them – a billionaire collector of precious stones, perhaps? 'That's all films. What they would get would be a fraction, an absolute fraction,' said career armed robber Freddie Foreman. Ex-commander of the Flying Squad,

John O'Connor, agreed, adding: 'The *Mona Lisa* may be worth £200 million, but no one's going to pay 25 quid.'

The value of the Millennium Collection would perhaps be estimable through an insurance policy, but no one could afford to insure them. Marsh, the largest diamond insurers in the world, would baulk at the idea of insuring a priceless set of diamonds so that they could be displayed inside a tent in South-East London, the criminal capital of Great Britain, without armed guards on patrol twenty-four hours a day, seven days a week.

The press reported that the diamonds were 'thought to be insured for £150 million'. Yet a spokesperson for De Beers revealed that: 'The diamonds were insured under De Beers' master policy, which covers millions of carats of diamonds. We cannot discuss the details of our insurance arrangements and, as pointed out above, insured the diamonds under our master policy. No separate policy document exists.' So the newspaper claims for the value of the Millennium Collection were based on what they imagined the diamonds to be insured for. It is interesting, though, that De Beers did not consider their most valuable diamond collection worthy of a separate policy document.

One other way of looking at the value of the Millennium Star is by examining how much De Beers had invested in it. It was bought, some say, for a mere £400,000 from the tribespeople who found it. The cutting and polishing cost around £1 million. Looked at in this light, the estimate of £350 million for the collection of twelve stones seems a little on the high side. If the Millennium Star was sold carat by carat, its wholesale price would be a shade under £1.5 million.

So what price the Millennium Collection? The stones had no specific insurance. De Beers sold the Millennium Star to De Beers LV for an undisclosed amount, and although it is for sale in their new shop it has no price tag. De Beers needs the incalculable price tag for publicity, but no one can buy it if it's supposedly priceless. Surely, though, something that unsaleable is worthless?

The Diamond Geezers didn't think so. Neither did the Flying Squad.

10 – GATECRASHERS

'I feared for my life.'

A DETECTIVE CONSTABLE ON CONFRONTING THE DIAMOND GEEZERS

'I received confirmation for 7 November on the early evening of 6 November from Tony,' said Betson. 'Everyone went out to Old Coal Yard, and we put on our gear and off we went. Terry said that I looked like Bob Adams with the mask on, which didn't go down too well with Bob. The mood was excited if a bit tense, to say the least. Millman was joking that I didn't know my tides tables because we'd wanted to do it the day before, but the tides weren't high enough. But we were confident that this was going to work, and we were joking as we got ready that we had better not get nicked by the Dome staff for not buying a ticket. In fact my biggest fear was that I'd wake up one morning to discover that someone else had beaten us to the diamonds.'

That morning of 7 November, the Flying Squad's patience was stretched to the absolute limit. The Diamond Geezers were now being staked out by 200 very tense men and women, 100 of whom were armed with automatic weapons. They were anxious for the safety of the Dome staff, who were going about their business completely unaware of the potential danger. The Dome was also still opened as normal to the public, and although the vault would not officially open until 9.30 a.m. there was always a chance that a visitor or two might be in the vicinity when the gang struck (as it turned out, there were no visitors close to the action, only Dome staff). By now, many officers were beginning to doubt that the would-be thieves would ever follow through with their plan. But today nothing was going to stop the Diamond Geezers.

At 07.26 a white Transit van, registration number N770 AHE, towed the red-and-white speedboat along West Ferry Road on the Isle of Dogs. The van was driven by Terry Millman and the passenger was Kevin Meredith.

At 08.11 a white Ford Transit van with the registration C673 COR drove into the Old Coal Yard in Plumstead. The van was, according to Betson, driven by Tony. The JCB was parked in the engine shed.

At 08.39 a red-and-white speedboat was seen travelling east along the Thames towards the Dome. The skipper of the boat, Meredith, then crossed the river into Bow Creek, where he tied the boat up and waited.

'I thought I was driving a boat to pick people up. We set off for Bow Creek. At Bow Creek, I turned the boat around and faced the Dome. I kept the engine running. I had a phone call from Betson, confirming I was in position.'

At 08.43 the JCB and van drove out of the yard towards Plumstead. The JCB driver, Betson, was wearing a fluorescent waistcoat. The JCB travelled towards Greenwich, turning right into Anchor and Hope Lane, where it was temporarily out of the police's sight.

At 09.07 the JCB travelled along Bugsby's Way towards the Dome. It turned left underneath the A102 Blackwall Tunnel Approach and parked out of sight of the police. This is where Ciarrocchi, Cockran and Adams got out of the second white van and into the specially modified JCB alongside Betson. The white van carried on and disappeared into the traffic.

At 09.27 the JCB turned left into Ordnance Crescent towards the Dome. It stopped in Drawdock Road, just short of the Dome's perimeter fence. Meredith, waiting anxiously across the Thames, said: 'I got a call over the radio that told me there was a bit of a delay. Then after that, over the radio, I heard, "Five minutes, five minutes." I thought it was Betson speaking. I was told to wait for the next signal and then go over to the pier by *A Slice of Reality*.

'I was worried sick when I heard, "Attack, attack! Attack, attack!" I didn't know what was happening. I just went straight across.'

Meanwhile, in Bronze Control at 09.33, Dome chairman David James had lost patience: 'My thoughts just beforehand were that this was a lot of nonsense and was never going to happen, and I was on the verge of telling the police to get stuffed. In fact I said if these crooks are going to come after all of this then they are the dumbest bunch I've ever come across. Then I got up and went to the toilet and missed the whole thing. I was very annoyed, to say the least.'

At 09.34 the JCB crashed through a gate in the fence, flattening a concrete bollard as it went, and moved into the grounds of the Dome. It headed towards Gate 4. Betson said: 'This was it, now or never. Once we had gone through the gate, we had to go on. This was the point of no return.'

At 09.35 the speedboat crossed the Thames towards the Dome from Bow Creek. 'I was frightened,' said Meredith. In his confusion, Meredith had gone to the wrong pick-up point and was waiting a hundred yards further down from the beach by the Queen Elizabeth Pier. 'I simply mistook the piers,' he said afterwards. A spanner was already in the works.

Meanwhile, in the Dome, lighting technician Mike Shepherd couldn't have been any closer to the action if he tried. 'I worked nights and would finish at around nine in the morning. As luck would have it, on the morning of the heist some lights in the cabinets in the vault needed fixing. I was waiting by the door to the vault at 9 a.m., anxious to go home and get some sleep, but the security were taking their time to turn up to let me in.' Group 4 had already been to the vault that morning and had deactivated the door alarms and opened the doors to the vault by typing in a code number twice. This was normal procedure. It allowed the cleaners access to the vault so that they were able to wipe the cabinets clean of greasy fingermarks left by the previous day's visitors. But the only cleaners present that morning were eight men armed with buckets, mops, dusters and sub-machine guns. Sergeant Clive Drew confirmed that there were eight armed police officers disguised as cleaners. Little did Shepherd know, but at that moment dozens of armed policemen and policewomen were watching his every move, wondering if he was part of the dangerous and ruthless gang. 'The time got to 9.05, 9.10, 9.15. I was thinking that the day shift could handle this and turned to walk away.'

Meanwhile, just outside the Dome itself, the Diamond Geezers had a problem. Betson said: 'I was surprised to see that the shutter to the Dome was closed. I had to make an on-the-spot decision.' Thoughts rushed through his head. He was not going to fail. He could not afford to. There was his family, debts, Marbella – and the rest of the Diamond Geezers were counting on him. There was too much at stake. This was his last chance. Determined that nothing would stop him this time, Betson made his decision. Gritting his teeth, he rammed the shutter, which, with a resounding crash, crumpled instantly. Betson was struck by some debris, which broke his nose as he drove through, but adrenalin overrode the pain as he turned the JCB towards the vault. Mike Shepherd counted himself lucky: 'As I was walking away, there was a bang and the JCB came through the shutter. If I had waited any longer, I would have been at the door of the vault when the robbers arrived!'

Betson didn't see Shepherd but did see what he later claimed to have assumed were two members of the corrupt security team. He headed in their general direction. 'It may have appeared as if I chased people, but I saw two Dome workers – one may have made a gesture at me – and they started running in front of our machine. I thought they were running with me.'

The two workers that Betson referred to were actually armed police officers. One of them was Detective Constable Carol Brocklesby: 'It [the JCB] was travelling quite fast and had a large bucket on the front. I couldn't see into the cab. I ran to the left and out of the way, and it followed my route. If I had not got out of the way, it would have hit us.'

Her colleague was Detective Constable Hayward: 'It was coming directly towards me. I shouted at DC Brocklesby, who was a few feet ahead of me ... if I had stood still it would have hit me. I shouted at DC Brocklesby to alert her and let her know what was going on and for her safety. At the closest the JCB was fifteen to twenty feet away. I was scared and had to take limited action to run away from the point of view of danger. I feared for my life. I was certainly, it is true, anticipating a JCB entering the Dome, but we did not know where it would come from and when it was going to happen. We had our backs to where the JCB came in ... I do not recall seeing anybody else at the time or any member of the public around at the time. I thought the JCB was trying to run us over and we could have been killed.'

'I pulled up outside the jewellery vault,' said Betson. 'Cockran and Adams got out and went into the vault. Aldo followed but stopped at the entrance to the vault.'

Once inside the Dome, Betson passed Joanna Eagan, who was one of the few non-police personnel present that morning. Miss Eagan was working as a host and had stepped out of an office to see what the noise was: 'I opened the door as a JCB came towards me. It was about twenty yards away, not very far. It came rushing through, a bit like a tank. I couldn't see a driver. I thought he was a bit out of control. I tried to see at the side if the driver was all right ... he was five or six feet away when he passed me. I didn't actually have to move to get out of the way ... it then stopped very abruptly.'

All three were wearing gas masks, but Adams was the only one not wearing body armour apart from Meredith and Millman. Millman was waiting patiently, having a cup of tea (with a dash of rum) from a Thermos in the getaway van across the Thames. Adams and Cockran entered the vault while Ciarrocchi kept watch outside and deployed the smoke grenades.

Ciarocchi said: 'I felt nervous and on edge. The first impression was confusing. The vault was shut and no one was about. I pulled one of the smoke-screening devices and I threw it down.'

Jason Forrest was working as a chef near by: 'At first I thought somebody crazy was trying to destroy the Dome. I ran out and saw the JCB as it turned left. Another guy in the cab had jumped out dressed totally in black, and he started throwing three or four canisters on the floor and smoke started to come out.'

Inside the vault, at 09.36 Cockran dashed to the cabinet containing the 203-carat Millennium Star. He fired into the glass with the loaded Hilti gun, and there was a loud crack as the nail went through, making a small hole. He quickly fired again, making another small hole. Adams then, perhaps releasing a lot of bottled-up anger, put everything into swinging the sledgehammer with all the strength he could muster. The first swing left the toughened glass cracked like a thin sheet of ice. Adams took a second swing, and to his amazement the sledgehammer went through the glass, making a fist-sized hole. 'I was twelve inches from payday,' he said later. 'I couldn't believe I had smashed the glass so quickly.' Cockran, meanwhile, had already set about the larger cabinet containing the Star's eleven blue satellites. A series of tiny holes were made across the glass. Adams, with a determined yell, swung the heavy sledgehammer another five times.

Meanwhile, in Bronze Control Shatford's deputy, Detective Inspector Swinfield, and Detective Inspector Williams, who was in charge of the firearms officers, received the confirmation that the Diamond Geezers were at the vault. They both looked at Shatford and nodded. Shatford then gave the order to arrest the suspects. Radios burst into life and the police leapt into action.

'They appeared out of nowhere,' said Shepherd, who was watching from a short distance away. 'Police were jumping out of rubbish bins, guns came from prams; it seemed as if there were hundreds of them. They pushed my friends and colleagues to the ground, screaming: "Stay down! Stay down!"'

At 09.37, outside the vault, Ciarrocchi was still igniting the smoke grenades. Detective Constable Beckton was the first to reach him. He said: 'The effect of throwing the smoke grenades scared me. It also covered what was going on. I used my weapon to cover Ciarrocchi.

Once he loosed the grenade, I couldn't see his hands and I pointed the gun at him.'

Ciarrocchi was quickly overpowered and arrested. When searched, he was found to be carrying further grenades, a Catherine wheel firework and a small Vicks nasal spray (30 millilitres) containing household ammonia.

Betson was still in the driver's seat. Police Constable Stephen Amis pointed his gun at him and shouted: 'Armed police! Armed police! Show me your hands!' Betson was then covered by another officer. Amis said: 'Show me your hands! Get out of the vehicle!' Before he could move, Betson was pulled from the vehicle and was pushed to the ground, face down.

'I shouted: "Out, hands in front of you!" But he did not comply,' said Amis. This is a particularly tense situation. If a suspect fails to show their hands or totally submit to an arresting officer, the police deem it acceptable for that officer to shoot the suspect, even if they are unarmed. A specialist armed undercover policeman later said: 'You are given a gun with blanks at training school and some massive thug walks towards you. Your commander tells you to stop and arrest him. You tell the thug: "Stop! Armed police!" They keep walking, you repeat it again, he keeps walking, now he's only six feet away, and a second later it's too late, he's got you. The training officer says: "Why didn't you shoot him?" You say because he wasn't armed. "But you're dead now, aren't you? This thug has killed you. Next time pull the trigger." Same if you can't see their hands; you don't know if they're trying to get to a weapon or have an explosive device. You're told: "If you can't see their hands and they won't show you, then you have the right to shoot to protect yourself."'

Police Constable Oliver joined in the arrest of Betson: 'I shouted: "Armed police! Show me your hands!"' And he put his right foot on Betson's neck and shoulder area, believing, mistakenly, that Betson was armed with a gun. 'I shouted: "Show me your hands!" He didn't reply.' However, Betson wanted to obey but couldn't pull his hands out from under him. His already broken nose was being further crushed by the policeman's weight, and he couldn't speak as his teeth were scraping the concrete floor. With a final effort, he eventually managed to pull his hands out from under him. Plastic handcuffs were put on Betson, who was by now bleeding profusely from wounds to the face.

Police Constable MacCauley then had the honour of saying to the leader of the Diamond Geezers: 'I am arresting you for attempted robbery of the Millennium jewels.'

With the suspects outside the vault safely detained, armed officers moved towards the vault itself. PC Martin was the first to take a look: 'I saw a man appear on the corner of the vault wearing a respirator with a torch strapped to his forehead. I pointed my gun at him, challenged him and shouted: "Armed police! Stay where you are!" He immediately ducked around the corner out of sight, and at this point the ballistic shield came to the front of our group and they used distraction devices, stun grenades.' The ballistic shield was used to protect the officers from the force of the powerful grenades.

The man who had ducked back around the corner was Bill Cockran, who immediately realized the game was up: 'I threw myself flat on the floor and put my hands out in front of me, so I would not get shot.' Then with a concussion-inducing '*Whump!*', two stun grenades went off by his feet and he lost consciousness. Covering each other with their weapons, the officers rapidly entered the vault.

PC Rodgers said that he thought Adams was lying on his hands, and when he did not show them he struck him several times with his right foot on the upper part of his body: 'Because I thought he was armed. I kept shouting: "Armed police! Armed police! Release your hands." But he didn't respond. PC Atkinson and I kneeled on him and managed to force his arms behind his back so he could be plasticuffed.'

'Well, of course, we couldn't answer. We couldn't hear a thing because of the stun grenades,' said Cockran afterwards. 'I was actually unconscious and Bob [Adams] was no spring chicken, he wasn't going to recover that quick.' One of the effects of stun grenades is to deafen and confuse enough to make it hard to hear and comply with the most simple of instructions.

PC Tiller said: 'I covered him with my gun. I jabbed him with my foot under his arm to make him release and show me his hands and he was physically restrained. He had spots of blood on his face, and I summoned a medic, PC Owen, to come and deal with him.'

As they handcuffed Adams, they noticed a strong smell of ammonia and discovered that both he and Cockran were carrying bottles of the substance. The officers then found that Adams was having difficulty breathing because one of the bottles of ammonia in his pocket had been broken, most likely because of the officer's boot, and he was suffering from the effects.

Meanwhile, armed officers deployed on three boats left their hiding places and moved towards the Millennium Pier. Any hopes Meredith might have had of escape were quickly dashed when he saw three boatloads of armed officers all pointing loaded guns at him. Sergeant Drew shouted, 'Armed police! Stand up! Do not move your hands!' and pointed a gun at Meredith. He was talked into the police boat. Sergeant Drew was plasticuffed to him. 'At 9.42 a.m., I leaned over the suspect and informed him he was under arrest for conspiracy to commit armed robbery and cautioned him.' Meredith seemed to have some doubt as to whether he was in fact told at that stage what he was being arrested for.

Terence Millman was on the north side of the Thames at the Lower Lea Crossing. He was parked in the white Ford Transit van (N770 AHE), which had towed the speedboat earlier that morning.

'I'd almost given up on Millman,' said Shatford. 'It was a case of knowing that he would be across the river somewhere and looking to find him ... We saw roughly where the boat was launched from and spotted Millman with the road signs out. 'No Entry' signs had been placed at the entrance to the slip road by Millman to make sure no one drove down towards the river, blocking the escape route. We then found the radios that were in contact with the rest of the gang.'

Millman was philosophical about the whole thing. 'Do you mind if I finish my tea first?' he said.

Inside the Dome itself chief executive Pierre-Yves Gerbeau and chairman David James rode down to the scene in buggies. 'The thieves were all on the ground trussed up like Christmas turkeys,' said James.

'It was relatively calm, and they were joking with the police, who were standing over them with guns. About 150 yards away in the central area there were 96 Miss World contestants taking a photocall. This was *Monty Python* stuff. The only complaint we had was from a party from Devon who were seriously miffed that they had not been allowed to see it.'

James was also pleased to point out: 'They [the Diamond Geezers] came on site when they were planning the robbery and they were paying us £20 a time.'

While the Flying Squad were arresting Betson and co. in Greenwich, officers from Kent picked up Lee Wenham and his father James at Tong Farm, where they also arrested a third man, Wayne Taylor, and charged him with assisting in the planning of the raid.

The Diamond Geezers were taken to different police stations in South-East London, including Greenwich and Plumstead (officers from Greenwich had actually assisted the Flying Squad with their investigations), for questioning.

Elisabeth Kirsch was at Ciarrocchi's flat, listening, fascinated, to the radio news coming in of the dramatic robbery attempt. She was looking forward to seeing Ciarrocchi that night as he had said that his money worries were almost taken care of and had promised to take her somewhere special to celebrate. There was a knock at the door. To Kirsch's utter amazement there were about a dozen policemen standing in the hallway. They handed the dumbfounded young lady a search warrant: 'Words cannot describe what I felt,' she said. 'Aldo hadn't mentioned a word to me about it. If he had done, I would have told him not to do it. I didn't even know if he was alive.' Later that evening, when they should have been drinking champagne in a candlelit restaurant, Ciarrocchi called Kirsch briefly from the police station.

On the following day, 8 November, the Diamond Geezers were formally charged with the attempted robbery of the De Beers Millennium Collection.

Operation Magician had worked ... or so it seemed.

11 – THE TRIAL, PART ONE: A GOOD START

'We were stuffed before the trial had even begun.'

RAY BETSON

The driver of the white van that had dropped Ciarrocchi, Adams and Cockran off under the Blackwall Tunnel Approach had somehow managed to evade arrest. Despite all the police surveillance, the driver could not be seen clearly and was therefore never identified. The vehicle was never traced.

Sergeant Clive Drew said: 'Efforts were made to find the vehicle, but it slipped through the net.' Detective Chief Superintendent Jon Shatford claimed that they didn't follow the van because criminals 'have a sixth sense and would have known that we were there'. Unfortunately for the Diamond Geezers, their sixth sense didn't alert them to the fact that they were being watched by 200 policemen. The white-van man was to feature prominently in the trial as the Diamond Geezers argued that this mysterious character, whom Betson named 'Tony', was working for the police and had, with the help of Michael Waring, set the whole thing up. The Diamond Geezers weren't going down without a fight.

But the trial was never going to be fair, in the opinion of the gang. As one robber serving time for a well-publicized crime said: 'The police latch on to cases that catch the public's eye, and obviously the more attention a case gets the more bird – nine times out of ten – you're going to get.' The Dome robbery had been covered in most national newspapers across the world. 'We were stuffed before the trial had even begun,' said Betson.

The trial was held in Court 5 at the Old Bailey, the smallest courtroom in the building, with poor acoustics and cramped conditions, which meant that it was often impossible for the defence to see the judge if they were sitting down. Martin Heslop QC, keen amateur yachtsman, headed the prosecution. Described as an 'awesome prosecutor' by a colleague, his most high-profile cases had been for work relating to casino licensing, drug smuggling and international law. His large, round glasses gave him the appearance of a wise old owl. This trial would be by far his most high-profile to date and would frequently see his speeches quoted in newspapers and on television across the world.

Oliver Blunt QC headed the defence, although each of the five defendants was also represented by his own legal team. His chambers, Furnival Chambers, say that Blunt, an enthusiastic rugby player, has 'a reputation for assured advocacy on heavyweight criminal matters'. He is also listed as one of the top leading criminal silks in London.

Judge Michael Coombe was the most senior judge in the Old Bailey – senior in every sense of the word, as he was called to the Bar back in 1957 and retired shortly after the Dome trial at the grand old age of seventy-two. He had a reputation as a feisty, tough, harsh sentencer of criminals, and his old-fashioned conservative values often clashed with those of the then Home Secretary, Jack Straw. He had complained to Mr Straw on a number of occasions when he was not able to impose as severe a sentence as he would have liked.

There ought to have been six defendants, but on 13 July, four months before the trial was due to begin, Terence Millman finally succumbed to his stomach cancer. He was fifty-six. He was being cared for in a hospice, and his passing was by all accounts 'peaceful'. 'No doubt he went with a smile on his face and a flask by his side,'

Ray Betson, the 'ringleader', his nose broken from the spectacular JCB crash, gives the camera the evil eye.

Terence Millman, a life-long criminal from South London, had worked with the best but needed one last big 'score'. The police described him as a 'good old lag'.

Aldo Ciarrocchi let off the smoke bombs to create confusion outside the diamond vault, but it was his dreams of a new life in America that went up in smoke.

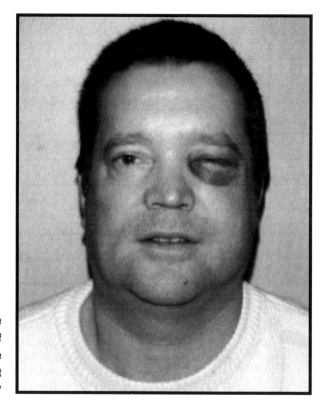

Bill Cockran's left cheekbone was smashed by the butt of a policeman's rifle but he remained chipper: 'At least we had the balls to try!'

Kevin Meredith, the driver of the getaway boat, was recruited the week before the final attempt. He claimed Cockran forced him to do it – but no one believed him.

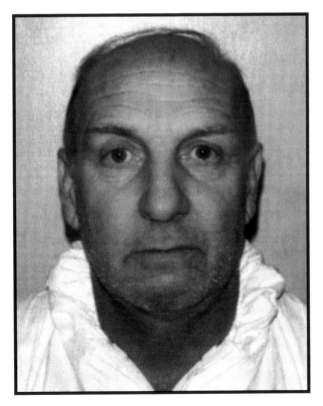

Remarkably, Robert Adams was only recruited the night before the raid. His tragic life came to a dramatic end in 2003.

The Millennium Dome, 'a white elephant', 'a giant contraceptive device', 'a carbuncle on the face of the millennium'. Whatever you call it, the £1 billion tent remains the most controversial building in the world.

The 203-carat Millennium Star; 'the most beautiful diamond I've ever seen,' as described by the former De Beers Chairman Harry Oppenheimer.

Lee Wenham: do not mess with this man. Wenham offered a very unusual bespoke service to the Diamond Geezers at his Kent farm (above right).

◄ The eleven fabulous blue diamonds, featuring the 27-carat Heart of Eternity (centre). Together, the twelve diamonds were said to be worth between £200m and £350m. Many believed they were worthless to thieves because they were unique. But one man thought otherwise...

Nobody wanted to catch the Diamond Geezers more than Detective Chief Inspector Jon Shatford – but was he motivated by a desire to protect the public or to salvage the Flying Squad's damaged reputation?

Betson and Cockran take the getaway boat for a test run. Millman paid for it in cash and signed the receipt 'Terry Diamond'.

It's off to work they go – the Diamond Geezers on their way to the Dome. Betson drives the JCB with the mysterious 'Tony' following in the white van.

'Twelve inches from payday' were the last recorded words of Robert Adams, who was reaching for the Millennium Star when the concussion grenades went off.

The glass was supposed to resist attack by hammer for 30 minutes, but Cockran and Adams got through it in an incredible 27 seconds.

'You can't park there.' The JCB outside the diamond vault.

The controversial body armour and gas masks – were they evidence, as the police suggested, that the Diamond Geezers had intended to use violence?

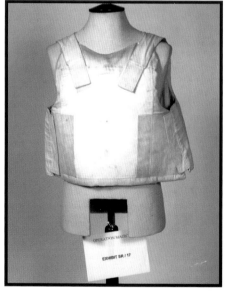

◀ The police thought the Diamond Geezers would be armed with automatic weapons, but the only shooter they found was this nail gun, used to weaken the glass.

said one ex-associate. The death of Terence Millman signified the end of an era. He was probably the last 1960s gangster still 'grafting' for a living. 'I spent time inside with Terry,' said Kray associate Tony Lambrianou, who was to follow Millman to his grave two years later. 'Nice bloke, lovely feller; good laugh was Terry.'

'He was what I would call a "good old lag [a habitual prisoner]",' Shatford said, smiling.

Robert Adams might as well have been dead for all the effort he put into the trial. His last publicly recorded words were spoken just after his arrest when he told a reporter: 'It would have been a blinding Christmas. I only hit the glass twice when it went. I cannot believe how easily it broke. Then that fucking mob came in and jumped on us.' He then refused to say another word. During the police interviews, Shatford said that Adams 'zoned out', and by that he meant that he 'was staring at a spot on the wall ... as if we weren't there'. Adams received no visitors when on remand, and he was hardly mentioned during the court case, except when Judge Coombe pointed out that he was brought in right at the end of the conspiracy and had 'never been picked up in the police surveillance'.

The boatman, Kevin Meredith, was not 'flavour of the month', according to one friend of the gang, because 'he sang like a canary, making up stuff to save himself' after his arrest before his solicitor told him to 'shut up'. This was much to the annoyance of interviewing officer Sergeant Clive Drew, who then called the solicitor 'a pillock'. The remaining three members certainly couldn't rely on his help. Betson, Cockran and Ciarrocchi would try to defend themselves as best they could.

It was up to the prosecution to prove their case. The Diamond Geezers had admitted conspiracy to steal, which carried a maximum sentence of seven years. They had, however, been arrested and charged with the more serious crime of attempted robbery, which is theft with violence and carries a maximum sentence of life imprisonment. The violence part of robbery is defined thus: 'A person is guilty if he steals, and immediately before or at the time of doing so, and in order to do so, he uses force on any person or seeks to put any person in fear of being then and there subjected to force.' The problem with British law is that in its efforts to be fair it often leaves certain aspects ambiguous, in particular in this case as to what exactly constitutes weaponry and fear.

Judge Coombe, after stating that the jury must return a unanimous decision to satisfy the court, described the weapons issue thus: 'Were these items carried by the defendants weapons or not? That is one of the most important parts of the whole case.' Shatford said at the time: 'I was very surprised that they didn't have guns, our intelligence – and it was good intelligence – was that these men were going to be heavily armed ... I do think that they had guns thereabouts that we didn't recover, and for whatever reason they decided not to carry them on that day.' But no guns were found. To ensure a long sentence for the gang, the prosecution had to turn 'these items' into weapons. The objects that were alleged to have contributed to fear and violence were: body armour, Hilti gun, JCB, ammonia, gas masks, smoke bombs, stink bombs and, bizarrely, the Catherine wheel firework.

Betson was not hopeful. 'We were goners,' he said; 'we were never going to be violent. If I felt that we would have needed guns, I wouldn't have done it. But the Flying Squad wanted a success, a reward for its biggest-ever operation.' Indeed, the world's press was watching, and the onus was on Britain to secure a lengthy conviction to show the world that British justice worked. Seven years would not be enough.

Mr Heslop, in his opening speech, made it clear that no holds would be barred. He said the accused were members of a gang who intended to steal 'twelve extremely rare and valuable diamonds'. He added: 'They were playing for very high stakes. This was no ordinary robbery. Had they succeeded, it would have ranked as the biggest robbery in the world in terms of value. It could properly be described as the robbery of the millennium. It was planned professionally and carefully down to the last detail. The conspiracy was so well organized it almost succeeded.'

At the start of his testimony, Betson insisted that the court know his lengthy criminal record, hoping that this would work in his favour. If his record had remained secret, as was his right, the jury could have made the assumption that his criminal past was far worse than it was. It would also work against the claims of Shatford that they were members of a 'dangerous and violent gang':

Heslop: Just about your background ... how long have you been involved in crime?

Betson: On and off, for most of my adult life.

MH: Over the last fifteen years, how have you been making your living?

RB: Out of traveller's cheques, cigarettes.

MH: By that, you mean dealing in traveller's cheques, or cashing them, or both?

RB: Cashing traveller's cheques.

MH: You actually go and cash?

RB: That's right, yes.

MH: Acquiring the cheques from other persons?

RB: That's correct.

MH: The cigarettes, do I take it you include booze in that area
as well?

RB: Yes.

MH: Is this knocked-off booze or is this duty-free?

RB: Duty-free.

MH: Can you help us? What sort of money are you making out of this?

RB: Yes, quite good money.

MH: Yes. Your last serious conviction was in 1985? For handling a quantity of stolen traveller's cheques and attempted deception, and you were sentenced to a term of eighteen months' imprisonment?

RB: Yes.

MH: You have not had a serious conviction since then, have you?

RB: No.

MH: So for the last fifteen years you have been actively working as a criminal, and I am not meaning to be offensive, but I just want to understand you, and have not been caught?

RB: Yes. Not every day of the week, though.

Judge Coombe: Sorry?

RB: I didn't say I was working as a criminal for the last fifteen years.

JC: I thought you did.

RB: There's been times during that period of time when I have been engaged in crime.

Judge Coombe later added: 'It is also right to say that he has never had any offence of any kind for violence or using violence.'

As for Cockran, Judge Coombe said that his crimes were 'mostly offences of dishonesty, burglary, theft, shoplifting, taking a conveyance without authority and handling stolen goods, and the last one seems to be 1992, nearly ten years ago'.

Speaking of Ciarrocchi, Judge Coombe said: 'Ciarrocchi had a conviction, but only one for shoplifting some time ago, and it was of Ciarrocchi that you heard a favourable report from the prison where he works for the Samaritans who have found him helpful and sensitive in carrying out their work inside prison and helping other prisoners.'

The court was satisfied that the defendants had no record of violence, apart from Adams, who had been jailed for six years in 1977 for attempted murder. Betson said that he called Adams because he could trust him and that 'he deserved a lucky break'. When asked if outside of the courtroom Adams 'was a bit of a psycho', Betson laughed and said: 'Not at all. He just doesn't get on with his ex.'

The trial livened up from the moment Ray Betson hit the stand. As the 'ringleader' and planner-in-chief of the raid, Betson was crucial to the weapons issue. His cross-examination by Heslop was the verbal equivalent of Muhammad Ali versus Henry Cooper. The silken words of the educated QC were rebuffed by the dyslexic wheeler-dealer, who would not be intimidated. This was much to the annoyance of Heslop but much to the court's amusement. One example of this was when Betson was questioned by Heslop as to whether the plan that was described in court was subject to too many variables, that too many things could have gone wrong when the JCB charged into the Dome:

MH: Did you not think that there might be a possibility that you would be delayed in some form or another?

RB: Did you think I was going to stop for a sandwich or something? How would I be delayed?

MH: Not quite, Mr Betson, with respect to you. The jury may be interested in your answers as to what you considered as part of this plan. The JCB might have stalled and you might have been delayed?

RB: It is a diesel engine, so they don't stall.

MH: It might have broken down?

RB: JCBs are renowned for their reliability and – may I just finish, please? I would like to respond, because you put the questions – we took the added measure of having it serviced a couple of months before.

As to the weapons, the prosecution made rather a lot of the Hilti gun but lost out to the defence when it was proven that this tool could not have been used, nor was it intended to have been used, as a weapon. Hilti guns were commonly used in robberies in the 1970s. They have recently gone out of favour, although a few robbers still prefer to use them, since they feel that the noise of the hammer smashing a protective screen instantly puts fear into victims while giving quick access to the tills. Judge Coombe subsequently dismissed the Hilti gun.

With regard to the body armour, the prosecution argued that it was worn because the Diamond Geezers were expecting to have to use violence, that people, either security guards or police, would try to stop them in the process of the theft of the jewels. Betson did a good job of explaining why he, Cockran and Ciarrocchi wore body armour:

MH: Why were you wearing the body armour anyway?

RB: Because when it came to the stage swap when we was going to do the swap for the diamonds and the money, it was just a bit of protection.

MH: What did you think was likely to happen?

RB: Someone could have pulled a gun on us – couldn't they? – at that stage.

MH: Who?

RB: Tony's people, who we didn't know, who was turning up with the money.

MH: I thought you said you trusted Tony fully?

RB: Yeah, I trusted him fully as far as the job was concerned, but now that we've got the diamonds it's a different thing, isn't it?

MH: So you thought—

RB: I trusted him as far as thinking that he wanted to get us in a position where we got the diamonds and nothing would go wrong with that, but now having the diamonds I just took this as a bit of added protection.

MH: So you trusted him on the basis that he wanted you to be successful and then provided you with the information accurately?

RB: Yes.

MH: But you also realized that there was a possibility he might double-cross you?

RB: Or if not him, the guy who he was bringing with him, who I've never met, who was bringing the money, or purporting to bring the money.

MH: Just explain to the jury what you thought might happen at this meeting at the Mayflower that was likely to make body armour beneficial to you?

RB: They could have pulled a gun on us.

MH: Do you mean you thought you might get shot? Let us put it in context. Not pulling a gun on you; you thought they might shoot you?

RB: Yeah, there was a possibility of that, yeah.

MH: That can be the only reason for having the body armour?

RB: There was a possibility of that, yeah.

MH: You thought there was a real danger, such that you were prepared to wear this body armour all the way from Old Coal Yard and in the course of the offence – a real danger that they might shoot you?

RB: I thought it was a possibility, yeah.

MH: A real danger?

RB: You use your dictionary and I'll use mine. I thought it was a possibility.

MH: I thought we agreed there had to be a real reason to wear the body armour in the first place?

RB: I have agreed with you on this, Mr Heslop, haven't I?

MH: So what did you do, apart from having body armour to protect yourself, confronted with that real possibility?

RB: What did I do?

MH: Did you take along a weapon to defend yourself?

RB: Of course not, no.

MH: Why not?

RB: Because I didn't.

MH: Just think about it, Mr Betson. If you are expecting a possibility that your colleagues may shoot you, it is one thing to have on body armour in case they do. You might actually take a weapon with you to defend yourself?

RB: I don't use weapons.

MH: You were prepared to go to a meeting in which somebody might shoot you and the only precaution you took was to wear body armour?

RB: It was a possibility they might.

MH: What if they shot you in the leg?

RB: Why do they sell body armour? I couldn't get body armour for my legs, could I?

MH: You see the point, Mr Betson? If there is any truth in your story, not only would you have taken body armour, you would have taken something to use by way of a weapon, if only to defend yourself?

RB: If I thought like you I would, but I don't think like you, do I?

MH: But you are a professional criminal. That is the point. You are not naive in this field. You know how these things work. If there was a word of truth in this story, I suggest you would have taken a weapon to defend yourself?

RB: You may well have done, but I didn't.

MH: I know you did not. I am asking why not?

RB: Because I don't take weapons. I don't carry weapons. It was an insurance that if someone had pulled a gun out or done something, I could run off, and I suppose it was like only probably in my thinking like a 10 per cent chance that would happen.

Adams and Millman didn't wear body armour, Millman because he was to wait in the van while the swap was done, as was Adams, who would have surely joined them in wearing the armour in the Dome if they were expecting serious resistance. Ciarrocchi said: 'Basically, we had to put them on straight after we got the diamonds, so it was more convenient to put them on first. After all, we might run into the police over the other side of the river, and the police might take a pot shot at me, so I was happier in body armour.'

In Judge Coombe's words: 'So much for the armour.'

Ciarrocchi also carried the smoke bombs and the Catherine wheel. Judge Coombe asked, rhetorically, in his summing-up: 'What purpose it may be used for; was it in order to make fireworks and frighten people or was it wholly irrelevant to the theft?'

Ciarrocchi said he found the Catherine wheel on the floor by his flat and he took it not to add to the equipment but because he hoped to use it when they celebrated the successful theft. It must have seemed to the jury that Ciarrocchi was a walking practical-joke shop as he also carried stink bombs. Heslop argued that the stink bombs were to be used to frighten tourists and staff. He said: 'Probably, in view of the smoke being generated and by them wearing gas masks, it was to facilitate an impression that some noxious substance was being used in order to keep people away.'

Betson said: 'I recall Aldo showed them and said something about dogs. It was said quickly in conversation. I didn't ask him what he meant.'

Ciarrocchi said that they were to deter police dogs. In the words of Judge Coombe again: 'So much for stink bombs.'

The smoke bombs and gas masks were rather more relevant to the crime. As Judge Coombe said as he addressed the jury: 'The point is you have seen the men in masks. Would they in fact cause people to have fear if there were people about? Was part of the reason, and the Crown suggest it was, to terrify those who were victims or possible victims if it were necessary to inculcate fear into the people in the Dome in order to accomplish the theft at the time of the theft, or immediately before?

'The next item is the smoke grenades or screens. Now, of course, the defence case is that they expected to be carrying out this robbery, sorry, this theft — the defence case is theft and not robbery at all. They were carrying out this theft when nobody was to be about, with the possible exception of some of Tony's friends, who were corrupt and on the wrong side of law and order.

'So they did not have to disguise themselves from any people, but they did have to worry about the fact that there would be videos. They realized there would be videos in at any rate some parts of these buildings if not all, and that was why smoke devices were carried.

'All the tools, said Cockran, were supplied by Tony or Terry, one or other, and the smoke was a screening device ... I assume that they were aware that everything would be seen by the video.

'The Crown say did they need screening devices of that kind? Also, the masks; were not the masks sufficient to distort features on any video film?'

Ciarrocchi confirmed that Cockran said the smoke bombs were screening devices, and he tried one out in a place near where he lived to see how effective it was: 'They were simply to screen us from the cameras so that nothing could be seen through the smoke, and we planned to drive out from an empty Dome.'

The prosecution even thought to produce a medical expert who was an authority on the chemical contents of smoke bombs. This seems a little extreme, even desperate, as at the most this would be an indirect consequence of using the smoke bombs and would not represent the intention to harm anyone who was in the area. Dr Kim Simpson said that the smoke bombs were: 'A type of commercial pyrotechnic composition consistent with a coloured screening-smoke-type formulation, and they are used in both military and civilian applications. They are used to obscure a target from an observer. They would generate large quantities of dense smoke, generally for use outside, rather than inside a building.

'In a confined environment, they could pose risk to people [and cause] respiratory, eye and skin irritation, and many of the dye materials used in smoke compositions are toxic when inhaled. Hence, exposure to this smoke in a confined area could lead to respiratory failure.'

However, the one thing the Dome is not is a 'confined area'. The Dome is the biggest building in Europe in terms of volume. The Eiffel Tower lying on its side would easily fit inside the Dome. So much for the smoke grenades, and so far, so good for the Diamond Geezers.

12 – THE TRIAL, PART TWO: A BAD END

'If there had been anyone behind that door they would not have stood a chance.'

WITNESS STATEMENT

The defendants were doing well up to this point. Betson's legal-aid solicitor, David Turner, said: 'All in all, we did a good job on the weapons issue, even with the ammonia.'

The Diamond Geezers said that the reason they carried the ammonia was to spray the surfaces of the vault, JCB and boat to eliminate DNA evidence.

Heslop: The procedure was that they would spray these areas before they left the vault to ensure there was no DNA?

Betson: That was the plan, yes.

MH: Does it strike you as a bit odd they would spray with these tiny bottles?

RB: The fine mist has an incredible amount of coverage.

MH: I suspect most of the jury know how these sprays work, using them as normal nasal sprays. You have just over 30 millilitres in these, and you have to spray all this glass cabinet, do you not?

RB: Bob had two, didn't he?

MH: Yes?

RB: And Bill had one.

MH: Even that would not be enough to spray all these areas, would it, to ensure that you got rid of all the DNA that was likely to be there?

RB: Of course it would.

MH: Why?

RB: Because it comes out in a fine mist and you just spray it and it is coated.

Cockran said: 'Ammonia was to be used for decontamination to spray with. We wore the gas masks in case any of it got into our faces, but they also served as masks.'

'I was going to spray the cockpit of the boat,' Betson explained. 'My gas mask was in the JCB, and I was to take that for the boat.'

Ciarrocchi's version tied in. 'I was to spray the cleaning fluid ammonia at the back of the JCB to kill any DNA,' he said. 'Ammonia was given to me on 6 October the first time, and it was then stored in the van. It was never going to be used as a weapon, and I actually suggested Mr Muscle as an alternative. In fact, when I mentioned Mr Muscle I was told not to complicate things by Betson. We were to spray on what we left behind. I pointed the squeezy bottle at no one.'

The defendants did not contest in any way the dangerous nature of the household ammonia, normally used as a strong cleaner. A typical bottle in the UK is 9.5 per cent ammonia and 90.5 per cent water. For domestic use, about 20 millilitres has to be diluted in 5 litres of water. They (allegedly Tony) had poured the ammonia undiluted into their containers; it was between 8 and 15 per cent proof.

Linda Vicker, a scientific officer, provided a written statement for the prosecution which explained the effects of ammonia being sprayed into someone's face: 'It causes a chemical reaction, and the severity will depend upon the volume and concentration of ammonia coming into contact with the tissues of the face. It is the cause of the most severe medical burns encountered in medical practice because it can rapidly destroy the cell membranes or boundaries, where the usual layers of the body are rendered useless. Ammonia can penetrate deeply into the eye, and it destroys the protective layers so readily. It is a vicious instrument of assault and can lead to cataracts.'

It does seem slightly unusual that the Diamond Geezers and their legal team did not contest this. Household ammonia does not actually burn skin when spilled, and the bottles the Diamond Geezers were carrying were so small and hidden so deep in their pockets that they would have been ineffectual against a determined security guard or police officer. A fast pair of legs would be better than waiting for the target to get close enough to be sprayed. There is certainly no question that ammonia would damage the eye if sprayed directly into it, but with the bottles that they were carrying the spray would be directed over a wide area and perhaps would not be concentrated enough to damage the eye. However, Judge Coombe did make it clear to the jury that the Diamond Geezers were correct in saying that ammonia would remove DNA and that 'none of the defendants drew ammonia when arrested'.

The timing was also an important issue, as the Diamond Geezers said that the raid was timed so that no one from the public would be around. This might not be hard, you may think, considering the appalling attendance figures at the Dome. In September they had been the lowest of the year, at 389,729 for the month (the New

Millennium Experience Company, responsible for the running of the Dome, predicted a minimum of a million a month). But even so there were witnesses who testified that some people might have been present. After all, despite the disappointing attendance figures, around 12,500 people a day were visiting the Dome. It was a question of how many visitors would be present when the Dome opened and, more important, whether any member of the public would have made it to the vault in the Money Zone, which was quite a way from the main entrance, by 9.30 a.m. Records show that there were sixty-two visitors to the Dome at this time and that they would have had to have jogged straight to the Money Zone to make it to the vault at the same time as the Diamond Geezers.

Another reason why the timing was so crucial was because the Diamond Geezers planned to be clear of the Dome before security could arrive. The starting time would have to coincide with the tides and a time when the place would be relatively or completely empty except for those who were involved in the conspiracy.

Betson said: 'We were going to use the pier next to *A Slice of Reality*, nearest to Gate 10, and there we were going to use a beach where a boat would be available. We wanted to use that beach, but it depended on the tide. The actual area outside the jewel house would be closed to the public until 9.30 a.m. There wouldn't be any maintenance people about and so it was safe to go in.

'We worked out how long it would take for security and then police to arrive on the scene. When the system was tripped, it'd go straight through to Hatton Garden [i.e. De Beers]. They would notify the Dome, and because I believed that there wouldn't be any security anywhere around the outside of the vault containing the millennium jewels – obviously, they had to come from Bronze Control or the security compound – by the time they responded to that we would have been gone ... We were also told that Group 4 don't come up and directly intervene in any criminal situation, such as a theft, or anything like that. They just call out the position over their radio and then it's dealt with by the police.'

Betson's arguments had made good sense up to this point, but then he got into difficulties with the witnesses who testified that they were in fear of their lives, with particular reference to his driving of the JCB. JCBs may not at first seem to be the choice of vehicle for the professional criminals, but recently diggers have been used in robberies. The first recorded use of a JCB (named after its inventor, J. C. Bamford) as a thieves' tool was in February 1991. A 7.5-ton digger was used to ram through the wall of an off-licence and tobacconist shop in Sydney Street, North Shields. Six men helped themselves to cigarettes and booze. A rather more ambitious gang struck in 1992. At 3.30 a.m. the Abbey National in Hempstead Valley Shopping Centre, Gillingham, Kent, had its cash dispenser ripped out by a JCB. The gang got away with about £50,000 after driving off with the 'hole in the wall'. On Easter Sunday in the same year, another Abbey National was robbed of £57,000 in the same way.

These thefts occurred when no one else was around. It is certain that if these gangs had attempted such a stunt in broad daylight they would have terrorized passers-by with the JCB. This was essentially the prosecution's argument, that Betson driving the JCB into the Dome created fear among those present. Betson said that there was constantly lots of building work going on around the Dome and that a JCB looked inconspicuous as well as being a good ramming vehicle. There was a concrete bollard in the way of the gates into the Dome that would have to be 'bulldozed' by the Diamond Geezers so that they could get into the part of the Dome where the diamonds were stored.

Since, according to Shatford, 'this was the largest Flying Squad operation ever to take place', it meant that there were more people in the area of the vault than would be expected normally. There were nearly sixty officers in close proximity to the vault. Police officers were, of course, the nearest to the action when Betson drove the JCB into the Dome, so there were plenty of witnesses who would say that the sight of a JCB driving into the Dome was pretty frightening. And unfortunately for the Diamond Geezers, the aluminium shutter they had previously always seen open was closed on the day. Their solicitor, David Turner, believed that the police had deliberately closed the shutter in an effort to secure the Dome. Betson said: 'On all [other] occasions when I went [to the Dome], the shutter was open.'

Shatford disagreed: 'Sometimes it was open, sometimes it was closed; more often than not it was closed. It's possible that on the days they looked it may have been open, we don't know. But we had no idea that that was where they were going to go in. It didn't have that much relevance to us.'

Lighting technician Mike Shepherd, who didn't testify at the trial, confirmed this: 'The shutters weren't predictable. I think they were usually open, but sometimes they were closed.'

On the day, Betson had to crash through the closed shutter. Although perforated and not particularly heavy, it made a terrible racket when it was rammed and led to far more fear in witnesses than if the JCB had been able just to drive in. As Joanna Eagan, a Dome host, said: 'I think the echo of that noise probably made it worse.'

MH: When you approached the shutter, which was down, did you think this was very odd?

RB: Yes, I did, yes, but—

MH: But what?

RB: I had to make a quick decision and I—

MH: You had reached ... I am sorry.

RB: I had to make a quick decision and I was being encouraged over the radio and with hand signals that it was OK.

The police witnesses would have been well briefed as to what to say in order to best help the prosecution. As one ex-undercover detective said: 'Police giving testimony would do so just to help the case. It's like finding an unloaded gun under the seat in an armed robber's car and putting a couple of shells in it. It's better to say in court that we found a loaded weapon. In the case of the Dome robbery, I would have said that I was in fear of my life, even if I was not, if I thought that it would help secure a conviction.' The evidence from the officers closest to the JCB was very damning.

> MH: Do you accept the evidence of two officers, Carol Brocklesby and Hayward, that you drove at them?

> RB: I drove towards two people who were dressed in the Dome uniform, who I thought were with me.

> Brocklesby: If I had not got out of the way, it would have hit us ... I was scared ... I made no reference to this in my witness statement, but the witness statement is more an *aide-mémoire*. I can remember perfectly well how I felt on the day without having to record it.

> Hayward: If I had stood still it would have hit me ... I feared for my life ... I thought the JCB was trying to run us over, and we could have been killed.

Then there was also the Dome staff:

> Miss Enver (host supervisor): They had something in their hands. I thought it was a gun. I was scared. I was frozen on the spot for a second. There was a lot of activity and I ran.

She also said that she saw two people running away from the JCB who had to get out of the way or otherwise they would have been run down. These were the two police officers, Brocklesby and Hayward. Other witnesses backed this up.

> Julia Hawkins (Dome staff): The JCB stopped and then started again. I was shocked and worried about the two people. I thought

they might get ... or I was concerned they might get mown down by the JCB.

Jason Forrest (chef): Stuck between the robbers and the police, it was nerve-racking to say the least.

Malcolm Wood (the Dome's security manager): I realized it could be a raid. I heard the vehicle crash through one of the doors ... I feared for my own safety and those I was looking after. We hid. I heard it go through the shutter. Dozens would normally be about in this area. I was apprehensive. It wasn't possible to arrange for every member of the public to be out of the way.

Some of the witnesses were more helpful to the defendants, but they were in the minority.

Sebastian Mow (Dome staff): It came to a stop about six feet away from me ... I didn't feel as frightened as a lot of my colleagues because I didn't feel I was in too much danger because of the heavy police presence.

But with so many police officers on call as witnesses for the prosecution, testimonies such as Mr Mow's would have little sway.

Cockran and Betson had slightly different things to say about the witnesses when giving evidence.

Cockran: I do not accept the evidence of a number of people that were frightened. I do not accept the lady's evidence that it looked as if we were out of control. It was all a controlled thing. I do not accept the fact that anybody froze on the spot ... I would not be frightened of a JCB. They go at 20 miles an hour, and I would not be frightened.

Betson: I've got a mixed view, to be honest, on the witnesses that came forward and the testimony that they gave. There was a couple of middle-aged ladies who I felt were sincere and genuine, and they seemed that they was shaken up and they was frightened. All I can say is that wasn't in our plan. I didn't envisage that was going to happen. I didn't drive directly towards them. I couldn't see them at the time, and I'm sorry that that was the case. But obviously that wasn't what we agreed to do. That wasn't what we thought would happen. We thought the area was going to be empty.

When I say my views were mixed, then when you've heard the other side of the equation, as you well know, there was people there, witnesses that were brought forward, that didn't put anything about being frightened or anything about being terrified in their original statements which were made at the time, and then they come up twelve months later in the box and they've got this sort of like emotional remembering, and now they're terrified. I mean, there was one young lady – she looked like Jennifer Lopez – and she was like ... she didn't put nothing in her statement saying that she was frightened at the time. She came up here and said she was terrified. Then she said that she was at a bus stop three months later and she saw another JCB and she was terrified all over again. I mean, she deserves some sort of an Academy Award, really.

There were some problems with the witnesses, and even the judge made the suggestion that it was the fault of the defence to not at least try to question their credibility. Eyewitness statements are notoriously unreliable, and English law had recently been changed to take this into account, as it used to be possible to secure a conviction on eyewitness testimony alone.

Judge Coombe: Of course, it is only right to remind you of the point made by more than one defence counsel I think in their speeches. Some of these witnesses whose evidence I have endeavoured to remind you of in the last quarter of an hour, eyewitnesses, had not actually expressed their fear and so on in their original statements. Is it the case, as the defence suggests, that they have exaggerated deliberately or unconsciously after the event?

The evidence of Mr Monroe [Dome staff] was read, and it was assumed until rather later in the trial that his evidence was not in dispute, but later on we learned from one of the defendants that it appeared to be very much in dispute and you will wonder why he was not called to be cross-examined.

In his statement, Mr Monroe said: 'All of a sudden there was a large crash. We looked to our right and I could see the yellow JCB digger smash through the gates. I think it was Gate Number 4. The gate went open and the JCB went through at speed. I was pretty shaken by this. I knew they were after something; they were approximately 50 feet away and I could see everything clearly. The JCB smashed through at speed Door 6. If there had been anyone behind that door they would not have stood a chance.'

That last sentence was crucial. Mr Monroe was the only witness who was not a police officer to state categorically that he believed that the Diamond Geezers could have killed someone at that point. He continued:

'I saw the JCB do a little left and right and then out of my view. I had a clear view of this as it was going away from us. Myself and a man called Richard ran through Door 5 of the Dome ... as we got down, I looked left and saw the JCB digger had stopped outside the jewels exhibit, facing us. I could see it all. I was scared. I didn't know if they had guns or not.

'The JCB engines were still running. Three men jumped out, and two went into the jewel exhibit ... they were wearing cream, off-coloured white scientists' suits.' [Mr Monroe was probably referring to the 'evidence suits' that police put the defendants into after the arrest. They were seen in these suits in the newspapers and on television. During the attempt, only Adams was wearing an off-white top and trousers; the rest of the Diamond Geezers were wearing casual, mostly dark clothing, i.e. jeans and jumpers etc.]

'Another male [Ciarrocchi] jumped out of the driver's cab on the right side. He had a full-face mask that he was carrying [Ciarrocchi was actually wearing it]. I was shitting myself. I didn't know if it [the smoke produced by the grenades] was toxic. We started to try and get people away. Throughout it all, I was scared not only for my safety but all members of my staff and the public.'

Unfortunately for the Diamond Geezers, Mr Monroe's evidence went unquestioned by the defence. The prosecution was back on top.

The mysterious Tony caused quite a few problems for Betson. Betson said he was told by Waring that Tony had worked as a Group 4 security guard at the Dome and had been sacked in February. Tony was said to have done all sorts of things, but in essence the defence argued that he had helped the police to set the whole thing up.

During the trial Betson said: 'My belief is that Tony set me up. Michael Waring was definitely involved. It may be that Tony double-crossed us. Perhaps Michael was going to claim a reward, and perhaps the Flying Squad set it up. Maybe Michael and Tony were doing it independently ... I believe that Tony was working jointly with the police to up it from theft to robbery.'

Neither Waring's nor Betson's stories wavered in court. Betson accused Waring of having helped him set up the job. Waring appeared as a prosecution witness and flatly denied any involvement of the kind Betson was suggesting. The prosecution did not accept any of the possible conspiracy theories relating to informants or inside men. When Shatford was under cross-examination, he refused to discuss police methods used in this case, particularly regarding informants: 'I will not be drawn on the questions in relation to informants at all,' he said. But Shatford admitted that they were not always 'one step ahead' of the Diamond Geezers and implied that they did not rely on informers in this case to any great extent.

The jury were bound to believe a decorated police constable rather than a self-confessed criminal who had been convicted of offences that involved deceit. That was all they had to go on, as the defence had failed to produce any further evidence to support Betson's claim that Waring put him in contact with Tony.

Despite this, Betson once again proved he could hold his own against Heslop, who argued that if Betson had relied on inside help, then he must have wanted to know who was going to help him:

    MH: You see, I suggest that the first thing you would have wanted to do would be to know at the very least who the staff were.

    RB: Why would I want to approach the staff?

    MH: They might be fifteen-year-old lads who were completely unreliable and on drugs all the time. I am not being facetious.

    RB: You think people like that would work at the Dome?

    MH: I do not know.

    RB: They probably did, actually, the way it was run.

    MH: We had some pretty elderly security guards, and you actually laughed at them on 1 September, because they appeared to be so ineffectual.

    RB: If you need to use that against me in your case, I mean—

    MH: I want—

    RB: No, you put it to me, so get the police officers to bring me the relevant video and let's have a look at it again and see if I'm laughing at old security guards.

Unfortunately, referring to this alleged conspiracy at all may have damaged the gang's chances of being convicted solely for conspiracy to steal. Judge Coombe said to the jury in his summing up:

'Members of the jury, it is just worth reflecting on this. What would be the point of Waring and Tony setting up a plan whereby Betson and the others would think that they could steal in peace with no one around? What would be the point of that if they were going to alert the police to the fact that this thing was going to happen?

'First of all, it would mean that Waring and Tony did not get any richer. What conceivable interest do they have in setting up a plan which was doomed to failure? That is something which you may think has never been really explained, although there are some suggestions it would be good for the Flying Squad and possibly even to bring a little news and cheer to the Dome as far as its financial takings were concerned, but what is in it for Tony and Waring?

'That is one of the matters you have to ponder over with care.'

This could be taken by the jury as a clear suggestion from the judge that Betson's claims were not worth noting and that Betson was lying.

Incidentally, with regard to the judge's suggestion of 'news and cheer' it is interesting to note that visitor numbers to the Dome in October were 657,624. In November, the month of the raid, the figures dropped to a record low of 387,103. This may suggest that contrary to popular belief, the raid did not cause people to 'flock to the scene' (as reported in the popular press) but made people stay away in droves, because the one thing the raid did make clear was the terribly inadequate security at the Dome.

Then there was the allegation of 'duress' made by boatman Kevin Meredith. Judge Coombe said: 'A working definition of duress, which has been given in the past by one of the Law Lords, is this. "It denotes such fear produced by threats of death or grievous bodily harm if a certain act is not done," and then these important words: "and overbears the wish not to perform the act, and is effective at the time of the act, making the man concerned to perform it."

'The threat of harm does not have to be made to the defendant personally. If he had a real fear of the harm coming to his wife and children, that could indeed, and no doubt on most men would, act as a similar force. Could the defendant have avoided the effects of the duress by escaping from the threats without damage to those members of his family who had been threatened because the law makes it clear that a defendant cannot say that he could not avoid the effects of the duress if a reasonable person would have done so?'

The answer to the judge's question was yes. Meredith had plenty of time on Saturday after Cockran approached him. On the Sunday he had ample opportunity to leave the flat, as by then it had certainly occurred to him that he was mixed up in a criminal enterprise of some kind. Judge Coombe asked: 'Would a reasonable man have taken it, providing of course that the police would agree straight away to provide protection for his wife and children? Nothing stopped Meredith from going off to the local police station or going to the local telephone box and dialling 999.' Meredith even said in his own evidence that Cockran was not that threatening and seemed 'perfectly reasonable' on Sunday, Monday and Tuesday.

Meredith's brother, who was called as a character witness, said that if Meredith's debts to Cockran had required urgent repayment, then he would have helped. Although it would have taken him a week to raise the money, he said he would have done so gladly in order to help him.

So much for Meredith. Or was it? As it happened, Meredith took up a surprising amount of the investigations, along with Tony, the security at the Dome and the revelation that Betson and his colleagues were not the first or last to want to relieve the Dome of the De Beers diamonds. And let's not forget De Beers, who, among other things, failed to point out at the trial exactly how well travelled the Millennium Collection was in 2000.

But first the sentencing must be dealt with.

13 - SENTENCING

'I remember thinking that this would be funny if it were not so serious.'

CLERK AT THE OLD BAILEY, COMMENTING ON JUDGE COOMBE'S ERRATIC BEHAVIOUR

Although there would be long periods of nothing to do while on remand, life was never dull as a Category-A prisoner at Belmarsh. Betson was opposite Sheikh Abdullah El-Faisal, a supporter of Osama bin Laden, who was jailed for nine years for inciting racial hatred. El-Faisal used language, captured on videotape, which encouraged the murder of Hindus, Jews and Americans. Those words led to his prosecution, the first for more than a hundred years, under the Offences Against the Person Act 1861. He said things like: 'If you see a Hindu walking down the road, you are allowed to kill him and take his money.' El-Faisal had studied with one-eyed, hook-handed Abu Hamza at the Finsbury Park Mosque. Hamza was subsequently arrested for his own extremist views, in particular his support for Osama bin Laden. Raymond Betson was so impressed with El-Faisal's solicitor, Muddassar Arani, that he eventually hired her to handle his appeal.

Betson's cell was also near Nicholas van Hoogstraten, the multimillionaire landlord convicted of hiring assassins to stab and shoot to death a business partner (though this was later overturned).

Van Hoogstraten was, and still is, widely hated by many people, including his tenants. For some peculiar reason he has a particular hatred for country walkers, referring to them as 'the scum of the earth' in a BBC interview. He also hates his tenants, an odd thing for a landlord to do, considering they provide him with his vast wealth. 'Tenants are filth, by their very nature,' he said in the same interview to a bemused reporter. Van Hoogstraten was released on appeal in December 2003. In the next cell was one of the Real IRA bombers responsible for the blast at the BBC Television Centre in Shepherd's Bush.

Cockran crossed paths with Great Train Robber Ronnie Biggs when they met in Belmarsh. Biggs was just beginning his sentence after returning from Brazil and turning himself in. Cockran was then on remand waiting for the Dome trial to start. 'He didn't mince his words,' said Cockran. 'He gave it to me straight that I should expect to go down for "a bloody long time" even if we could prove we were in Rio on the day of the Dome job.'

Meanwhile, in another part of the prison, Meredith seemed to be unable to stop offering people lifts in his boat. The prison service was shocked to learn that Meredith went on a fishing trip with some of his jailers. Meredith accompanied warders on two boating trips while on bail. He took six jailers he had met while on remand on his father's 30-foot launch on 4 November 2001. He went on another trip with five warders on his father's second boat on 12 January 2002. At the time, a prison service spokesman said: 'This is a very serious matter. There will be a thorough investigation.' On 24 July 2002 seven prison officers were sacked as a result of the investigation surrounding Meredith's boating trips.

It almost seemed as though Meredith was taking advice on social behaviour from his fellow prisoner, the disgraced novelist and peer Jeffrey Archer. Meredith befriended the celebrity convict, and they got on so well that Archer gave him a mention in his *Prison Diary*. In his book, the disgraced politician recalls his barrister's advice never to believe anything he is told in prison, but adds: 'Kevin is so courteous and kind that I really do want to believe him.'

At the Old Bailey, the jury spent seven court days deliberating. Judge Coombe had requested that the verdict be unanimous, but the jury were unable to agree. Finally, Judge Coombe said that he would accept a majority verdict. The next day, before a hushed court, the jury foreman announced that they had reached a majority verdict of ten to two and that they found the Diamond Geezers guilty of conspiracy to rob the De Beers Millennium Collection from the Millennium Dome – except for Meredith, that is, whom they found guilty of conspiracy to steal but not to rob.

Sentencing took place on Monday 18 February 2002. The average sentence for robbery in the UK is 6.6 years; the maximum sentence for theft is 7 years. Sentencing, Judge Michael Coombe said: 'A value was placed on the diamonds of some £200 million. You played for very high stakes and you must have known perfectly well what the penalty would be if your enterprise did not succeed.'

Then it became clear that the defence had indeed wasted time, money and effort on the accusations made against Police Constable Michael Waring and the mysterious 'Tony'.

'I am not going into the evidence about inside men, except I think it is only fair to say to the police officer who was called that as far as I was concerned it was quite apparent that he played no part in it. What else may have happened, I simply do not know, but whether there were inside men or not, and whether you were led to believe that few people would be about as opposed to many or not, the fact is this was a wicked plan, a professional plan, and one which was carried out with the most minute attention to detail.

'I must deal with this as a wicked and highly professional crime. There is no doubt on the evidence that you, Betson, were in this from the earliest possible stage, and that you were responsible, possibly with others, for the initial planning. Stand up now, William Thomas Cockran and Raymond John Betson. On Count 1 of this indictment, conspiracy to rob, you will go to prison for eighteen years. Let them go down.'

Betson smiled wryly as the judge passed sentence. Cockran pulled a painful grimace.

Judge Coombe continued: 'I come now to you, Aldo Ciarrocchi. I do accept first of all that you came into this later, but as early as 1 September, two months before it took place. You are entitled to rely, as the first two defendants were not, on your relatively good character. The only convictions against you were really ones I can totally ignore for shoplifting, so I treat you as a man of wholly good character.

'You were tempted into it, I have no doubt, by the others. You knew the risks you were taking, but your good character and the fact you were not in it from the beginning must, I think, mitigate a little the sentence which I have imposed upon the other two. I also take into account that you are a relatively young man. You will go to prison for fifteen years. Let him go down.'

Ciarrocchi bowed his head. He couldn't meet Elisabeth Kirsch's horrified eyes.

'I accept in your case, Robert Alvin Adams, that you were a latecomer to this. You cannot pray in aid, as Ciarrocchi could, fundamentally good character. Although you have not been in very serious trouble – and the trouble you were in was serious enough, by any manner or means – for some time, you were prepared to play a key part in this, and in all the circumstances I think it would be proper to give you the same sentence as Ciarrocchi, namely fifteen years. Let him go down.'

Adams grinned as he was led away to the cells, the first public display of emotion since his arrest.

And as for Meredith, well ...

'You, Kevin Peter Meredith, have been acquitted by the jury of Count 1, but convicted unanimously of Count 2; in other words, the jury have wholly rejected the pathetic defence of duress you have put forward. I think in my many years at the Bar and the Bench, I have never heard a defence of duress with less merit or less substance. In all the circumstances, you will go to prison for five years.' At this, Meredith's wife and mother both burst into tears in the public gallery. Meredith sobbed as he was led away, but he was almost instantly released, having served nearly enough time while on remand to be eligible for parole.

Twenty-five-year-old Elisabeth Kirsch, Ciarrocchi's girlfriend, really had something to cry about, but she swore to a *Daily Mail* reporter that she would stand by her man. The fifteen-year sentence, she says, has been devastating. 'It is my worst nightmare come true. It hasn't changed my attitude towards him or our relationship. Financially, I'll be fine because I have never relied on him. But emotionally it will be an uphill struggle. Is he worth it? If I didn't think so I wouldn't hang around. Some people say he doesn't deserve me, but I know how happy he makes me. When I get into bed at night, I still cannot believe he isn't with me. I miss him so much, but I'm trying to get on with my life as best I can. I don't stay at home every night, but I am absolutely not interested in other boyfriends. The trouble is that if anything good or bad happens to me, he is completely helpless to do anything about it. He has let me down, but more than that he has let himself down.'

She continues to see Ciarrocchi as often as possible, despite the humiliating experience of visiting him in jail. 'There are so many security checks because he is a Category-A prisoner. I have to remove my coat, shoes and jewellery. I am thoroughly searched twice, which includes looking in my ears, mouth and nose. We meet in the visitors' room along with other inmates. A guard sits next to us. We can hold hands and kiss. I find public displays of affection difficult, but I am not inhibited verbally. We also write three or four letters a week to each other and talk for about twenty minutes every night on the phone.'

On their third anniversary, a hot day in August 2001, Kirsch was visiting Ciarrocchi. She told him that she felt so sad that they couldn't enjoy the day together. 'Suddenly he pulled the ring from his Coke can, got down on bended knee and loudly asked me to marry him. Everyone in the room heard, and some started crying. I said "Yes" straight away,' said Kirsch. 'He did it to make me happy. It was so sweet and thoughtful.' While the happy couple come across as quite naive, in the greatest irony of all they have demonstrated quite clearly that any 'ring' can be used to declare everlasting love. One can only assume that no diamonds will be present at the wedding.

'Aldo is coping all right inside,' said an ex-convict who had recently visited Ciarrocchi. 'He's fit and well. He's working in the prison library and doing an A level in English.' He's also working for the Samaritans again, trying to help other inmates who are depressed or suicidal.

'I smiled when the sentence was given because I'd expected it,' said Betson, 'and I wanted to scream "I told you so" to the court, but nobody was going to listen. I mean, no one had heard the truth about us. Then, with all the fuss over, that's when it starts sinking in a bit. When the remand is over, that's it, your time has really begun and you know you ain't gonna see your family and friends for a long time, particularly when you're sent miles away from home. I ain't gonna see my boy for a decade, maybe more, as we seem to be being made an example of.

'Surviving jail is not easy. There's a lot of suicides and it's very easy to get depressed. If you've got family, then they can help, visit and write. In my community there is a network of people you can call upon for help, friends and colleagues, that sort of thing. You just buckle down and get on with it. You exercise, meet people, work on the appeal. You feel powerless, though: your brief [lawyer] is out there with tons of cases and no time for yours; it's very frustrating. But I'm not whinging. That's just some of what's hard about doing time.

'It's a stressful experience. Look what happened to Adams. He was strong as an ox, but a year inside finished him off.' In a finale worthy of a Johnny Cash song, a few months into his fifteen-year sentence the sad life of Robert Alvin Adams came to a sudden end on 13 September 2003, when he suffered a massive heart attack. He was sixty years old.

The final key player to be sentenced was Lee Wenham, who was tried in a separate hearing. Despite being portrayed in court as an unintelligent man with an IQ of just seventy who had been lured into the plot by a gang of sophisticated criminals, Lee Wenham was jailed for four years for his part in organizing the Dome job and nine years for his role in the Aylesford robbery. Wenham's comparatively light sentence reflected the fact that, as prosecutor Heslop said: 'He played a knowing part in the preparation for the Aylesford attempted robbery and in the reconnaissance and preparations for the Dome. But he is not a key organizer, and his role was down the chain to both offences.'

His father, James, was freed on the direction of the judge for lack of evidence. Wayne Taylor, 34, the third man arrested at Tong Farm and the only one to be charged but not held on remand, was freed earlier, also on the direction of the judge. Judge Coombe said there was no evidence that Taylor had been involved in the plot: 'Suspicion is never enough. There is no evidence he ever joined this conspiracy.'

Outside the court, Taylor said he was considering suing the police for wrongful arrest: 'I have been to hell and back being wrongfully arrested for something I did not do,' he said. Taylor was spotted visiting the Dome by the Flying Squad's surveillance unit on 22 September. But after the visit he was not seen there again (he didn't sue in the end).

Even before sentence was passed, however, there were already those in the court who felt that Judge Coombe's performance during the Diamond Geezers' trial was unsatisfactory. Throughout the proceedings, Judge Coombe reinforced some of the stereotypes that judges have become famous for, such as Justice Oliver Popplewell, who amazed the High Court by asking in 1998: 'What *is* in Linford Christie's lunchbox?'

Judge Coombe constantly referred to Millman as Merriman and dozed off intermittently during speeches made by both defending and prosecuting counsels. According to witnesses, he actually fell asleep during the closing speech made by the defence. On being told that Judge Coombe had dozed off, Martin Heslop QC said: 'Well, you can't really blame him.'

Two persons who witnessed the trial made statements to this effect. A *Panorama* journalist, who attended the trial almost continuously from November 2001 to February 2002, said in her statement: 'There were several occasions where what I saw and heard gave me the impression that Judge Coombe was asleep. I saw his head falling and lolling. On one occasion his head had fallen so far as to be almost in contact with the table. At other times I got the impression that he had woken up with a start. There were occasions where I also saw him sitting back with his head dropped low towards his chest, and I heard sounds which I would describe as snoring noises. Altogether, I would estimate that on approximately half a dozen occasions the judge was asleep ... I also recall that there was some discussion among some of those present in court about this matter.'

A court clerk said: 'During my time clerking the case, His Honour Judge Coombe fell asleep. I was totally shocked by it. It was not a few seconds of a doze. The judge would slump in his chair and fall asleep. Nobody tried to wake him. What seemed to wake the judge up was the sound of his own snoring. I remember members of the jury nudging each other to look at the judge while he was sleeping. I also distinctly remember two lady jurors shaking their heads in disbelief.

'On one occasion, it looked like one of the jurors had dozed off, and I told counsel who was sitting directly in front of me. I then looked over to see if the judge had noticed that the juror had also fallen asleep. I remember thinking that this would be funny if it were not so serious.'

The QCs and solicitors have been reluctant to come forward, because they don't want to be seen as trouble and it's never good for a QC's career to appear as a troublemaker in court. The cramped conditions of Court 5 at the Old Bailey have also to be taken into account, as the counsel had a restricted view of the judge and wouldn't necessarily be able to spot whether he was sleeping. One can't help but wonder what the judge might have missed when he was resting his eyes. However, nothing was said at the time.

All in all, it seemed to be a good result for the Flying Squad. Shatford was asked whether he thought the sentences were fair. 'Yes, I think it's fair,' said Shatford, 'very fair when you look at the crime itself, in a public area, when the robbery would have been the biggest in the world effectively in terms of value, and there's got to be a deterrent sentence. So I think it's just.'

Interestingly, there has been very little academic research into the subject of armed robbery – almost none, in fact, apart from popular true-crime books. The only serious research in this country comes from Roger Matthews, Professor of Criminology at Middlesex University. A leading authority in the field, Professor Matthews has published four books on the subject, including *Armed Robbery* in 2002. As part of his latest project, Professor Matthews and his team interviewed 350 convicted armed robbers and spent some months with the Flying Squad.

When asked about the fairness of the sentences handed out by Judge Coombe to the Diamond Geezers, Professor Matthews said: 'Sentencing is a difficult issue. I would argue that the Dome robbers should have got five to seven years, but the sentences they received were "exemplary" sentences because of the notoriety of the robbery.'

Professor Matthews added: 'The failure of the British courts to take into account the ability and the intention of the "armed" robber to inflict harm on his victims means that, in practice, there is no disincentive for robbers to carry real and loaded firearms. Any rational sentencing policy would provide every incentive for robbers not to carry real and loaded firearms rather than justifying current sentencing policy in relation to the perceived threat to the victim. In general, greater consideration needs to be given to the intentions of the offender as well as to the potential threat to future victims.'

So it would seem that it was pointless for Betson and the gang to have hoped for a lighter sentence by going unarmed and when few people were around. Therefore, it would seem that despite their claimed consideration for others they were not given a reasonable sentence of five to seven years. What message are we sending to future robbers who spot a vulnerable target and might not be feeling as 'charitable' as the Diamond Geezers were to the general public?

Professor Matthews is not alone in this opinion. The Sentencing Advisory Panel, the official body that advises judges on sentencing, was set up to promote consistency in sentencing throughout England and Wales. On 10 April 2003 the panel said that sentences for robbery are too severe and that current thinking on robbery sentences, laid down in cases in the 1970s and 1980s, were out of date and called for a radical rethink.

The Court of Appeal is obliged to take account of advice from the independent panel, and it is expected to trigger the introduction of a new set of guidelines. The panel said robbery covered a wide range of circumstances. The violence could be as little as tugging on a handbag strap. Yet the crime closest to robbery in sentencing patterns is grievous bodily harm with intent, which always involves serious violence. Apart from robberies in the home, the current starting points for judges 'would be likely to appear too high'. The panel suggested new guidelines for all types of robbery, ranging from street muggings to organized heists, proposed four levels of sentencing, and noted that the new system would be 'likely to result in lower sentences than those currently approved by the Court of Appeal'.

Its chairman, Professor Martin Wasik, said: 'We propose that the degree of violence used or threatened should be the primary factor in sentencing robbery, taking full account of injury to the victim and the nature and duration of threats made. Ordinarily, the value of the property stolen will be given relatively less weight than the violence or intimidation. Where a robbery involves little or no physical injury to the victim, it is hard to see the additional harm involved in robbery that justifies sentencing levels comparable with those for grievous bodily harm with intent.' From these recommendations, it would seem that the Sentencing Advisory Panel is in agreement with Professor Matthews and would recommend a sentence of around five to seven years for the Diamond Geezers. All the Diamond Geezers could do for now was wait and hope that these recommendations were put into place by the time of their appeal.

This raises the question, though, as to why the Diamond Geezers went ahead with the attempt, unarmed, thinking that they could successfully achieve the world's largest theft in one of the world's most densely populated cities in broad daylight, and uninterrupted. Part of the answer lies with the company that was supposed to protect the Dome – a security force that had become famous for all the wrong reasons.

14 – THE COMEDY ZONE

'Saddam Hussein could have got in without paying.'

DOME EMPLOYEE

roup 4 was in charge of security at the Dome. Group 4 was, and
still is, one of the most controversial companies operating in
Britain. It has an annual turnover of about £1.5 billion and is the
world's second-largest provider of security and related services. In
recent times Group 4 has striven to position itself at the forefront of
the movement to privatize prisons. In the UK it runs three of the
prisons operated by the private sector and is responsible for a large
proportion of prisoner transportation. But its record over the past
fourteen years is filled with allegations of incompetence, corruption,
greed and neglect.

In March 1990 Norman Fowler, then chairman of the Conservative
Party, joined Group 4 as a non-executive director. When Fowler
resigned from the board in 1993, Group 4 founder Jurgen Philip-
Sorensen commented: 'Norman has been a personal friend for over
thirty years, and I have valued his wise counsel over the years.' The
day after Fowler resigned, Home Secretary Michael Howard
announced the second phase of the prison privatization scheme. Not
surprisingly, Group 4 won the first contract, worth £6 million, to
manage the UK's first privatized prison, Wolds in Humberside.

A little more than a year later, Judge Stephen Tumim, the Chief Inspector of Prisons, condemned the regime at Wolds. Complaints included 'corrupting lethargy' as well as a high incidence of violence and drug abuse. These words have haunted Group 4 ever since.

In 1993, just three weeks after taking responsibility for the first private prisoner-escort service in the country, Group 4 became a laughing stock when they managed to lose seven prisoners in one week.

In a separate incident in May 1993, a drunken prisoner, Ernest Hogg, choked on his own vomit while in the care of Group 4 Court Services. Hogg lay unconscious and unnoticed in the back of a prison van for several hours before he died. Group 4 were later found guilty of 'lack of care'.

In August of the same year, a Home Office inquiry criticized Group 4 for using excessive restraint in handling a female prisoner. Despite her asthma and low-security-risk status, she was handcuffed and locked in a van cell for two hours. Tony Blair, who was the Labour home affairs spokesman at the time, demanded that such a 'comedy of errors' be brought to an end forthwith. 'It is time for the Home Secretary to get a grip on the prison escort service and ensure public safety. If he cannot be satisfied that Group 4 are providing a service in an effective way, he must take steps for the contract to be withdrawn,' he said.

Less than a year later, a hunger striker who had been admitted to hospital from the Campsfield House detention centre managed to escape from under the noses of his Group 4 security officers. The Group 4-run government facility, based near Oxford, also saw hunger strikes and rioting that resulted in a mass escape over the perimeter fence shortly after it opened in 1993.

In September 1994 Group 4 agreed not to use excessive force at the Stanworth Valley protest camp after an injunction application made by Chris Maile and son Philip, of the local Green Party. In October of the same year, Philip Maile was hospitalized after a Group 4 security guard illegally used a pressure-point hold to the back of his head. He spent three weeks in a neck collar.

In March 1995 the inquest into the death of Wolds inmate Darrell

Barson ruled that he had committed suicide. Barson was on a fifteen-minute suicide watch but had not been seen for several hours before his death. The prison doctor said staff were too inexperienced to tell suicidal behaviour from signs of drug abuse and that 90 per cent of the prisoners he saw were 'drugged up to the eyeballs'. Between October 1999 and July 2001 Group 4 were fined £59,142 for poor services and for failing to meet basic standards at Wolds.

In 1996 Group 4 was at the centre of a corruption scandal at the European Commission in Brussels. It was alleged that Group 4 beat the twelve other companies competing for the contract to run the Commission's security because it was allowed to change its bid after the submission deadline. The investigation into the matter by the Commission found that there was 'strong circumstantial evidence' that the bid had been manipulated.

In August 1997 Campsfield exploded into a riot after some detainees thought one of the inmates was being strangled by Group 4 security guards.

Group 4's handling of detainees caused another outcry in 1997, when it emerged that the company had transferred a prisoner between vans on an M6 petrol station forecourt in full view of the public. In 1998 nine men were acquitted of charges of rioting and disorder at Campsfield after it was proved that Group 4 staff lied when they gave evidence.

In 1999 Group 4 was criticized for its running of Medway, a prison for young teenagers. The staff were found to have used excessive force (neck and wrist locks) to restrain the inmates up to 150 times per month. A report said that the centre was more likely to strengthen criminal behaviour than lessen it. A fine of £68,000 was imposed at Medway for failure of service and £638,000 was withheld by the government for services not provided at Medway and Wolds.

Between September 1998 and November 2000, Group 4 was fined an incredible £425,000 for its poor service at Altcourse prison in Liverpool, but even this enormous amount of money was written off by Group 4, which then made cutbacks at Altcourse, saving the company more than £14 million.

Group 4's role in privatization, and the mismanagement of privatized sectors, can in itself be seen as a corporate crime. If any doubt remains about the altruistic nature of Group 4's activities, the following quote from its annual report says a lot about the company trying to take over public services: 'Group 4 considers its most important social responsibility to be ensuring that the company has a good and sound financial position and preserves the ability to generate growth and create jobs.' On its website, the company boasts a personal reference from Prime Minister Tony Blair, made after it provided security for a meeting of Commonwealth heads in 1997. He said: 'I am very grateful for Group 4's help in providing an extensive range of security staff and equipment.'

And despite Blair's earlier reservations, his government awarded Group 4 the contract for the safekeeping of the most controversial public building in Britain, the Millennium Dome. Security was the top priority at the Dome, despite all the jokes about poor attendance and the lack of persons likely to be desperate enough to try to sneak in without paying. There was the fear, in Shatford's words, that 'there was a very real terrorist threat' to the Dome.

Group 4 collaborated with De Beers over the security of the vault in which the Millennium Collection would be kept. De Beers made a £2 million donation to the Dome. Much of that, according to their spokespeople, was spent on security to protect the diamonds. The diamonds were monitored with CCTV cameras by De Beers staff at their HQ in Charterhouse Street. The diamonds were also watched over by Group 4 security guards in their on-site office, Bronze Control. Inside the Dome, a staff member would be near the display at all times. Any attack on the armoured glass would trigger an alarm that would go off at all three locations. The diamonds were fixed into steel poles. To be removed, the gems would have had to have been cut loose with strong bolt cutters. Although the Metropolitan Police didn't actually patrol inside the Dome, a total of eighty-nine additional officers (including Michael Waring) were seconded to the Greenwich Borough Operational Command Unit to undertake high-visibility patrol, traffic patrol and crime investigation duties in anticipation of the increased numbers of people visiting the Dome and Greenwich.

It would seem, then, that the diamonds were well guarded. Getting hold of the Millennium Collection was not going to be easy — or was it? At the trial, Betson and Cockran described the security as 'a joke' and that it was 'an opportunity too good to be missed', 'the chance of a lifetime'. They also said that the vault was poorly guarded and that by the time any Group 4 security guards had arrived they would already be aboard the boat. These claims seem extraordinary in the light of the money that was and still is spent on the Dome's security. It costs £400,000 per month just to keep the Dome empty. From July 2001 to April 2003, £4 million was spent on security.

Yet dozens of ex-staff and visitors to the Dome believed that security was poor. Even prosecutor Martin Heslop QC admitted that the security staff at the Dome 'were elderly and pretty ineffectual', and during his cross-examination of Betson said: 'You might have had one of those on your team, and you wouldn't have been very happy, would you?' When speculating about why the Diamond Geezers didn't carry guns, Shatford hinted that in reality Dome security was poor. 'Quite why they didn't take them [guns] I don't know. Perhaps they thought that this is going to be so easy that we won't need them anyway,' he said. There were a number of security breaches at the Dome in 2000 and, although some workers said that breaches occurred 'almost daily', there is no public record, and nor will it ever be known just how many there really were.

One of the most famous breakdowns in security at the Millennium Dome occurred on its opening night. On 31 December 1999 more than 2,500 irate VIP invitees, in dinner suits and evening gowns, queued in the cold for up to seven hours to collect passes that should have been delivered by post. First, they whiled away a few hours outside Stratford station, which was eventually closed because a shortage of security scanning equipment made it impossible for organizers to cope with the numbers. While ten screening arches had been provided by the Metropolitan Police to the New Millennium Experience Company, only five had been erected on the site by New

Year's Eve. Incredibly, no one had thought to check that there would be enough room for them. This allowed just 625 of the 10,500 invited guests to be processed every hour. At Stratford there was only one scanner available to deal with up to 8,000 guests. The waiting luminaries included national newspaper editors, who spent the evening sharpening their pencils in anticipation of the following day's headlines.

One source, who does not want to be named, said that she was one of a team of people brought in to help with Dome security on the opening night. 'It was laughable,' she said. 'We were desperate to get people through because the stations were so overcrowded, and eventually people were pouring past us without having their tickets properly checked.'

Guests faced further delays when they tried to board special trains to the Dome. It was like Monday morning rush hour. Just when it was thought that it couldn't possibly get any worse, security equipment at Charlton station failed, forcing embarrassed officials to start ferrying guests to other already overcrowded stations, including Stratford. A public-address announcement at Stratford advised people to catch buses to board an alternative tube service. At 9.30 p.m., many remained stuck on the platform beneath a flashing sign which read: 'Welcome to Stratford, the Gateway to the New Millennium 2000.' Dozens were starting to make their way home.

'It was a nightmare,' said a Group 4 worker. 'I lost count of the number of times somebody said: "Do you know who I am?" I was terrified that something bad would happen during the opening ceremony and that it would be my fault for letting someone through unchecked.'

Mike Shepherd, the lighting technician who was at the vault door on the morning of the robbery, started work at the Dome in November 1999 and stayed until it closed in December 2000: 'For the first six months from when it opened, security was dreadful. Saddam Hussein could have got in without paying. After that it got a bit better but not much. I tested security by holding up a piece of grey card as a security pass to gain access and wasn't stopped. A colleague lost his pass and went to security and said that he was a production manager when he was in fact a general assistant. They gave him the production manager pass, no questions. It was crazy.'

As the Dome was mostly lit from above, the lighting technicians had to be pretty handy with a rope: 'We would have to climb and abseil down the roof of the Dome to install lights, and we had to tie each others' knots so you had to have a lot of trust. That makes you close friends.' You have to be specially trained to do this, and Shepherd and his colleagues had qualified with the Industrial Rope Access Trade Association.

Since they were the only ones at the Dome really qualified and authorized to go up to the roof, inside and out, Shepherd and his colleagues had a rather unusual task. The Dome had a particular problem with a peculiar kind of security breach. 'It wasn't hard to climb up on to the roof,' says Shepherd. 'Anyone could if they could get past the security guards, which couldn't have been hard because so many did. One guy was so angry at the Dome's cost that he clambered up on to the roof with a bucket of clothing dye in the middle of the night and wrote a bunch of random obscenities, which we had to go up and clean off.

'Sometimes we'd have to go up and get people down. As we worked at night, we would get the loons and the drunkards who had got it into their heads that it would be a great idea to have their picture taken on the roof of the Millennium Dome. One night, four young men in their twenties, who had obviously been out drinking, climbed up on to the roof and raced each other to the top. Their idea was to take a picture. I climbed up to get them down and ended up chasing them round the roof, which isn't easy considering all the safety harnesses I'm secured to. These lads, clearly drunk, had nothing to stop them from falling. The roof of the Dome is not a safe place. There are special vents and wires that are easy to trip over, especially at night.

'Eventually, they gave me the slip by climbing down and somehow managed to avoid the security guards on the ground. One, however, jumped down by *A Slice of Reality*, on to the beach there. The police came by in a motor launch but decided they didn't want to get their feet wet and let him get away — that is, if he didn't drown or sink into the mud there.'

Britain's most famous serial streaker, Mark Roberts, gatecrashed the Dome in June 2000. Roberts, thirty-seven, made televisual history when he jumped naked on to the floating weather map of Britain during the daytime television show *This Morning* in 1995. He has also struck at the Wimbledon finals, the Commonwealth Games in Manchester, the Rugby World Cup, the Grand National and the FA Cup Final. When I spoke to him, he'd just sprinted across Ascot racecourse on Ladies' Day and went on to streak during Superbowl 2004, but was famously upstaged by Janet Jackson. He has been arrested twenty-four times and been fined more than £3,500, although he has since won a lucrative advertising contract for a sports clothing company (he promotes trainers).

Each time Mr Roberts has streaked or attempted to streak, he was, eventually, apprehended by security guards and/or policemen — until he visited the Dome, that is. In November 2000 the Dome hosted Miss World. With an audience of 2.5 billion watching live on TV, it was the ultimate thrill for this unashamed exhibitionist. Armed with a tear-off tracksuit in a sports bag, he emerged from North Greenwich underground station at around 5 p.m. There were dozens of police everywhere, and when Roberts tried to get through he was stopped and told that the Dome was now closed to the public. After telling them that he was picking up tickets from the box office, he was let through and then just walked straight past the ticket desk and the security on the door, straight into the Dome.

'I couldn't believe how bad the security was,' said Mr Roberts. 'Once inside, I wandered around trying to find out where the contest was to take place. I went up to a coffee stand and asked the guy behind the counter and he pointed and said "Here". As I turned around, I saw a stage in the middle of the arena with seating all around. All I had to do now was find somewhere to hide until the contest started. Dodging behind the backs of two security guards looking the other way, I hid in a nearby generator room with four large holes at the front of it.'

From where he was, Roberts had a clear run at the stage. It was perfect. He noticed that he was covered in grease and muck from getting in through the hole into the generator room and changed into his working clothes (a dark tracksuit, loosely held together with Velcro). He was all set to go. But then it was announced over the Tannoy that there was a security alert and that everybody was to be evacuated. Not wishing to be blown up, he emerged from his hiding place.

'A security guard came over, but much to my relief didn't say anything about where I'd come from, which did seem a little odd. We were herded into two hospitality suites. After a few minutes, a lady came in and told us what was happening. There had been a coded bomb warning and they were checking out a suspect car in the car park. There was a bomb scare going on, and I was walking around in a dirty Velcro suit with a suspicious black bag over my shoulder, no questions asked.'

It got worse for Mr Roberts when he sat on a chair in a quiet corner, as his trousers split open underneath and at the back, leaving his rear exposed. 'After about twenty minutes, a member of staff came in with dozens of bottles of champagne, an attempt to make up for the inconvenience. I did a rush job on my trousers and went over to get a drink. If I was going to get arrested, I may as well be drunk.'

The ceremony was taking place on 30 November, just over three weeks since the attempted heist, and yet Roberts was standing, covered in dirt, in a torn suit with a black bag thrown over his shoulder, ticketless, his bottom hanging out of his split trousers, right in the middle of all these dignitaries who were supposed to be protected by the Dome security at one of the most controversial events of the social calendar. The story doesn't quite finish there, as on his way out after the all-clear, Roberts asked for some complimentary tickets. They gave him four. He is still hoping to add Miss World to his list of streaking events.

Roberts was not the only prankster to embarrass Dome security staff in 2000. Mark Thomas is a campaigning comedian who investigates multinationals and governments and exposes them on his TV programme, *The Mark Thomas Comedy Product*, which is screened on Channel 4. Disgusted at what he considered to be the tremendous waste of money spent on the Dome, he and a dozen friends decided to take their protest right to the Dome itself. The results were broadcast on his programme in 2000. The day was spent running rings around Group 4 security guards as they organized one protest after another, eventually having to improvise spontaneous protests as they managed to get away with much more than they had hoped to.

First, a crowd of 'homeless people' set up camp between the legs of the Body Zone, making the point that the money spent on the Dome might have been better spent on affordable or free housing. 'Security were having apoplexy,' said one of the protesters. 'There was one guy we christened "Blowjob" because he looked like he was the victim of a reverse liposuction experiment. I had a very interesting debate with the chief security officer about how long the homeless people could stay there, with a variety of answers.' The final stunt was held in the main arena where Mark had gathered a few dancers just before the main 2.30 p.m. show, and they'd managed to sneak on to the main stage in the arena while others were diverting the attention of the handful of security guards who had bothered to come and do their job. The dancers were all wearing T-shirts with a single large letter on them, and when they arranged themselves on the stage and opened their jackets to reveal the T-shirts the letters read: '£800 M QUID FOR BIG TENT SEEMS CRAP'.

The Millennium Dome being the huge worldwide attraction that it is, the protesters thought that it was also necessary to convey the message in French, German and Italian by cleverly reshuffling the line of people so that it read the following:

£800 M POUR CETTE MERDE, £800 M FUR DIESE SCHEIßE and £800 M PER QUESTO MERDA.

'One of the funniest moments of the day occurred just after this, as a couple of folk decided to have some fun with the security staff, lined up across the entrance to the zones. At one point they just legged it past the security guards into the Faith Zone and then split up and ran different ways. About four guards chased after them, lost them, and they just ran out the back and joined us again at the front a few minutes later.'

Perhaps the most shocking example of lax security is provided by eighteen-year-old Alex Jasionowicz, who worked at the Dome for eight months in 2000. He said: 'I would show people around. I started work at the Dome after studying tourism at a nearby college. It was my job to show tourists around the Money Zone and the vault where the diamonds were kept, to give them talks about the diamonds and help the visitors interact with the exhibits.' In April, Group 4's Dome security service manager Malcolm Wood made the host on duty responsible for the security of the vault, instead of a Group 4 guard as previously. But no one told Alex that he was now the first line of defence between the diamonds and any ruthless would-be diamond thieves.

But Group 4 must be doing something right because they are still guarding the Dome today. Unfortunately, they refused to participate in any official interviews for this book. Even Shatford was reluctant to speak about them. When asked how many Group 4 personnel were aware of Operation Magician on the day, he said: 'No one knew.' This was incorrect. Group 4 did know about the attempt from the beginning of September. They opened the vault on the day of the robbery and helped police keep a 100-yard cordon around it before the gang struck. Wood said that he met Shatford in early September: 'It was the first time I met Mr Shatford. Before that we had a few police officers in the control room. After the meeting it was decided to withdraw the host on duty from the outside of the vault for his own safety.' At this time the police also confirmed that Group 4 security staff would not interfere if there was a robbery attempt but would ask for police assistance.

Unfortunately, Group 4's reluctance to be interviewed for this book probably means that we will never know why it was decided to reduce the vault security from a Group 4 security guard to only a host between April and September 2000, or why people were able to go unchallenged into parts of the Dome that were not for public access. And why were brand-new Dome security uniforms thrown in skips? The Diamond Geezers were found to have these uniforms in their possession but had decided not to use them in the end. During the trial, Betson said in court that there were corrupt security guards in the Dome and that Tony had been one of them until he was sacked in February. Group 4 failed to conduct an internal review of their staff at the Dome. If anything, this would have helped the case for the prosecution and might have exposed Betson as a liar. Perhaps Group 4 was scared of what they might have found.

With security so lax and badly organized, it was no wonder that the Diamond Geezers believed that with a bit of planning they could steal the De Beers Millennium Collection from under Group 4's noses. And there are yet more tales to come of 'corrupting lethargy'.

But what about De Beers' role in securing the Millennium Collection in the vault? Surely they had made certain that their most prized possession was safe from the most determined of thieves? In actual fact it wasn't very secure at all, and nowhere near as well protected as it could quite easily have been. But then Betson would have decided to call off the whole job if he had known what exactly De Beers were up to in 2000.

15 – NOBODY'S VAULT BUT MINE

'It was unfair for people to be looking at the fakes, believing that they're real.'

A HOST WORKING IN THE DOME'S MONEY ZONE

De Beers stand accused of much worse things than Group 4. 'Corrupting lethargy' is distinctly small time when compared with some of the allegations that have been levelled at the gem-mining giant.

It costs De Beers on average £3.50 to mine a high-quality diamond weighing 0.8 carats. When cut, such a diamond is worth around £550. The weekly pay of an African mine worker on South Africa's Atlantic coast is about £6.60. For them, diamonds are not associated with love, as they are in the rest of the world, because they are not allowed to live with their wives in the diamond-mining towns. The same rule does not apply to the white diamond workers. Then there are the cutters. Some 80 to 85 per cent of the world's gem diamonds are cut for 10p to 15p each. The take-home pay of an Indian diamond cutter is a paltry £3.28 a week. The total cutting, mining and transporting of a stone for an average £800 engagement ring costs about £5.

As part of their strategy to maintain their global monopoly, De Beers buy up profitable diamond mines and close them down. One such mine existed in the unlikely-sounding location of Arkansas, USA. The owner of the farm who discovered the diamond mine on his land was bought out by De Beers with the promise of a high-paying job at the company. The farm is now a museum, and for a few dollars you can spend the day digging for diamonds. Bucket-and-spade tourist amateurs net around 300 carats a year. Mines in Africa have been turned into 'nature reserves' where animals are flown in by the Boeing-load to make up the numbers.

This practice has led to the forced displacement of the indigenous tribespeople of the Kalahari Desert in Botswana, Africa, where a rich diamond pipe was discovered in 1980 by a Canadian prospector. De Beers bought the land immediately and tried to hush up their 'investment' lest the local tribespeople made the not unreasonable demand for their rightful share. De Beers then discovered that the mine produced gems of such amazing quality that they simply had to mine it. And mine it they did. De Beers were able to pay off an impoverished Botswana government, and the Kalahari tribespeople were brushed aside to make way for yet another mining town.

Then there are the so-called 'blood diamonds', diamonds that are used to finance war. A few years ago De Beers feared an international consumer-boycott campaign by activists, who said that diamond trading fuelled civil wars in Sierra Leone, Angola and the Congo. Instead of opposing them, De Beers helped to draw up the Kimberley Process, a scheme backed by the United Nations for regulating and tracing the production of diamonds. Eventually, fifty-four diamond-producing countries were listed as part of the process. Others will be excluded from legal trading. This shrewd piece of politics dreamed up by the Oppenheimers bolstered De Beers' image while pushing aside irregular traders, which means that it also helpfully allows De Beers to keep a tight grip on the global supply.

Unfortunately the Kimberley agreement isn't worth the paper it's written on because it only bans diamonds sold by rebel groups, not by governments. Any government that exploits or violently oppresses its own people is excluded from the agreement, and so are free to sell diamonds to finance their despotic regime. And De Beers can easily break the Kimberley agreement thanks to their secret warehouse in the Free Trade Zone at Zurich airport. When blood diamonds arrive here from the world's trouble spots, such as Sierra Leone, Liberia or the Congo, De Beers 'export' these diamonds to Russia, for example. They don't actually go anywhere and remain in the warehouse until De Beers do the paperwork, legally *importing* the same diamonds from Russia. This means that they are now clean and can be sold on the open market. Such is the background from where the African-born Millennium Collection came, containing as it does diamonds mined from land once farmed by the Kalahari Bushmen as well as the Millennium Star, which was found during a bloody civil war in what is the most conflict-prone land in all of Africa, the Congo. De Beers claim that the Millennium Star was sold to them by Bushmen, but it is not known whether these Bushmen had connections with any rebel group fighting in the Congo at that time. Even if not, the Millennium Star is the biggest blood diamond of all time, bought as it was at the height of the Congolese civil war.

Whether miners in Africa or consumers in America, many people have cause to feel that they have been hard done by the diamond industry. And if you were a tourist in Britain who was looking forward to visiting the Dome to gawp for a few seconds at the world's most valuable diamond collection, then you could have been conned too, because for a large part of 2000 the diamonds weren't there. In 2000 the Millennium Collection went on a world tour. In February the twelve diamonds were in Paris, in March they were in Dubai and in July they appeared at the twenty-ninth World Diamond Congress at the Antwerp World Diamond Centre. On 8 September they left the Dome for the last time and were sent for a two-week stint at Tokyo's National Science Museum, and on 13 September they made their debut there at an exhibition called 'The Nature of Diamonds'. They arrived back in the UK on 30 September. By this time, De Beers had been informed by Shatford that an attempt was going to be made to steal the collection, so the diamonds were immediately squirrelled away at De Beers' offices in Charterhouse Street near Hatton Garden. Of course, immediately after the raid the media unquestioningly reported the information given to them by De Beers, which was that the diamonds had been moved from the Dome the day before the attempt when they had in fact left two months previously.

A De Beers spokesperson has since said: 'On all occasions [when the diamonds were away], apart from the last (at the request of the police), a sign was placed inside the display indicating that models were being used.' Being a host in the Money Zone was Alex Jasionowicz's first full-time job. A keen and conscientious young man, he loved his work but was shocked by the behaviour of the Dome's security staff. 'They [Group 4 security] would tell me on the day that the diamonds had left for another trip abroad, but they never put a sign up and no visitors were to be told. I thought it was unfair for these people to be looking at the fakes, believing that they're real.' But how are we to know that the real diamonds were ever in the Dome in the first place? It's not as if anyone would be able to tell. If you put a fake diamond behind thick glass, even the world's foremost diamond expert will not be able to tell the difference from a distance of only two feet. De Beers say that Alex is lying and that they would never be so 'dishonest'. Yet out of all the people who visited the Dome whom I have spoken to for this book, none has so far remembered seeing such a sign. Betson says he went to the Dome with Millman in July, when the diamonds were in Antwerp. If a sign saying that the diamonds were away had been up, could that have been the end of the Diamond Geezers' plans?

The vault seemed to be well protected. During the trial, prosecution barrister Martin Heslop said: 'They [the diamonds] were protected by very sophisticated alarms. The Star was in an armour-plated cabinet costing £50,000 to construct. The other eleven were in a similar cabinet.' Although £100,000 seems like a lot for two cabinets, it was a mere drop in the ocean out of the £2 million that De Beers had donated to the Dome for security. Indeed, one of the most striking things about the attempted heist was the ease with which the glass was smashed. De Beers tried to smooth things over by stating that: 'Apart from the robbers being able to break the glass, every level of security worked exactly as planned – for example, as soon as the glass was attacked the alarms were activated and the whole thing was seen on camera by De Beers' security officers, who were not aware of the plot.' The head of De Beers' security in London was Timothy Thorn. Speaking under oath at the Old Bailey, he said that breaching the cabinet should have taken at least thirty minutes. In fact it took twenty-seven seconds for Cockran and Adams to make a hole in the glass large enough for a fist to go through. Just after the police arrested him, Adams said that he was only 'thirty seconds from payday'. Cockran said the nails fired from the Hilti gun went through the glass like 'a knife through butter'.

David James, Chairman of the NMEC, expressed his total surprise when he heard that it had taken the Diamond Geezers only twenty-seven seconds to break through the glass: 'The vault was reputed to be very nearly impregnable, and it was very difficult to see how anybody could just go in and walk up and take the diamonds out of it. That was something that came as a huge surprise to me, and I rather suspect that it came as a huge surprise to a great many other people too.' Shatford said: 'I was surprised, yes. I'd been told that it was special reinforced glass that was meant to withstand quite a force, but they managed to get through very quickly.'

No glass exists that is unbreakable. Glass can delay criminals' attempts to get at goods, but that is all. The best glass to use to prevent or at least slow down smash-and-grab raids, according to the experts, is anti-bandit glass, a laminated glass made up of two glass plies bonded together by one thick plastic interlayer. The interlayer is designed to increase significantly the amount of time and effort required by an intruder to gain access through the glazing.

But according to a well-known specialist security-glass manufacturer, laminated glass cannot be curved. The Millennium Star was enclosed within a glass cylinder. When this was put to De Beers, they said: 'At the time of manufacturing the case, both De Beers and our insurers [remember the insurers were De Beers themselves] were happy with the security advice we had taken on the build and design of the showcase.' Thorn said: 'We were heavily involved in the design of the vault and with designing the display cases to meet high security standards.'

So what glass could have been used? 'A less efficient one,' said the glass manufacturer's representative. Essentially, to get a curved cabinet, it is possible to use the same glass but without the plastic interlayer. This means less protection from intruders using combinations of sharp objects like pickaxes and blunt objects like sledgehammers. Considering that the Hilti gun has been used in robberies since the 1970s, De Beers' security must have been aware that this glass was less effective. It seems terrifically strange that the world's most valuable diamond collection was not protected by the world's strongest glass. But for a few months in 2000 the glass didn't have to be the most secure on the planet, as it was simply protecting fakes. 'Yes,' said the De Beers spokesperson, 'they were made at the beginning of the year. It is standard practice for De Beers to make models of large diamonds, not for security purposes but as a record of the diamond.'

Rudolf Droeschel operates from a tiny workshop in the basement of his house in Idar-Oberstein, Germany. Using traditional tools, he specializes in the legitimate manufacture of fake gems for use in films, costumes, exhibition displays and so on. You name it, he's faked it, from the Hope to the Cullinans (the entire set of twelve), and had actually produced quartz copies of the Millennium Collection for his own enjoyment (his personal favourite was the 27.64 carat heart-shaped stone, the Heart of Eternity) by January 2000.

Droeschel said: 'I received a request from De Beers. I'd done work for them before, but they wanted the Millennium Collection in zircon because quartz wasn't of high enough quality and I couldn't do that, so I passed the job on to my colleague.' His colleague is the only jeweller in the world expert enough with zircon to do the job. The cost was approximately £2,000. If you'd like your very own copy and that's too expensive, you can order a quartz one from Droeschel for a reasonable £130. It's a very good likeness.

'They're a funny lot,' said Herr Droeschel. 'They asked me for all the paperwork, so I don't have any records of it now, but I remember it very well as it was such a peculiarly difficult job. Three times we were asked to do it: February, April and May 2000. Yes, they're a funny lot. No one else does business like De Beers.'

So there were plenty of fakes available in 2000, meaning that the Millennium Collection could appear at several locations at once, if De Beers felt there was the need. But why did De Beers need three copies? One was stored at their HQ in Charterhouse Street for their personal records, one for display at the Dome when the real ones were away and one for ... a spare, perhaps? You never know when you might misplace one. The fakes all have permanent homes now. On 12 December 2000 the Dome welcomed its six-millionth visitor. Deborah Ansell from Copnor, Portsmouth, accompanied by her two sons, was given a replica of the Millennium Star by bubbly French chief executive, Pierre-Yves Gerbeau. De Beers kept one for their own records. The spare one eventually went to the police. Anthony Oppenheimer, president of De Beers, presented a copy of the Millennium Star to Metropolitan Police Commissioner Sir John Stevens. It now has a permanent home within New Scotland Yard's Crime Museum (but don't try to visit as they won't let you in unless you are a serving police officer). Sir John said he was delighted to receive the replica on behalf of the brave and dedicated officers involved in the massive undercover operation. 'Catching the robbers responsible for the attempted Dome robbery was a huge success for the Metropolitan Police service,' he said at the ceremony. 'The efforts to pull off one of the largest robberies in the world in broad daylight were utterly audacious and worthy of a James Bond film plot.'

Perhaps the most remarkable fact of all is that the equipment to make the Millennium Star entirely secure was in place but was not operational. When the Millennium Dome first opened, many commented on the fact that the low attendance figures were matched by the long wait for exhibitions in the zones, so many exhibits were hastily redesigned to try to speed things up. Such was the case with the vault. 'The showcase was essentially a tube of glass,' the De Beers spokesperson said, 'allowing visitors to see the diamond [the Millennium Star] from all sides, with a brushed-steel tube over it which covered the section in which the diamond was being displayed. When visitors entered the display area, the diamond was hidden and was gradually revealed to them during a timed light show. The steel shroud would gradually be raised to the ceiling but would return to position at the end of each show.' The timed show was switched off because the NMEC was unable to manage the flow of people into the space, and the brushed-steel shield was never seen again. The shield was not mentioned during the trial. It would have been extremely simple to have arranged a system whereby a bang on the glass would have not only led to the alarm going off but also to the steel cylinder falling down, completely protecting the diamond in an impenetrable case.

The question now is: if signs saying that fake diamonds were being exhibited instead of the real ones and Betson or one of the other gang members had seen them, would they have gone for it? Betson and Millman visited the Dome during July, possibly at a time when the diamonds were in Antwerp. If the glass had been laminated polycarbonate, would they have gone for it? If they had known about the steel tube, would they have gone for it?

Betson takes his time replying. Eventually, he says: 'The steel tube would have been a decider if it had reacted to a bang on the glass and would then fall over the glass, protecting the diamonds. You can have all the heat and light sensors and alarms in the world, but it ain't going to do any good if the glass is easy to get through, especially if there are no guards. I reckon Bill could've still got through slightly stronger glass, but anything over ninety seconds and it would have been too long. If I had seen a sign saying that the diamonds were being exhibited elsewhere, I would've tried to discover the itinerary, but, thinking about it, that would be near impossible. You'd never know if you'd found them all out. So on the balance of it, no – I wouldn't have gone for it.'

Thanks to De Beers and Group 4, the Millennium Collection was a poorly guarded set of diamonds, so much so that any criminally minded person might think that they would have a decent chance of swiping them. So why didn't more criminals try? Well, truth is, they did.

16 – MEANWHILE, BACK AT THE DOME

'This is a prime example of what a shambles the Dome is.'

DOME WORKER AND WHISTLE-BLOWER, LEN O'REILLY

On 6 November 2001 the then chairman of the NMEC, David James, had agreed to a formal meeting with someone called Len O'Reilly, a former Dome employee, at the offices of the NMEC in Greenwich. O'Reilly claimed to have some important information which James should know about.

As one of Britain's leading 'company doctors', David James's job was to ease the Dome's transition from public to private hands at the end of 2000. The sixty-five-year-old, who prefers 'crisis manager' as a job description, has had plenty of experience in turning around ailing or collapsed companies, not to mention smashing illegal international arms-dealing rings. James played a key role in uncovering the Iraqi supergun affair in 1990. During a visit to one of the Eagle Trust's conglomerate's subsidiaries, he noticed a muzzle of what looked like a giant gun. He tipped off MI6, who enlisted James's help, and with the assistance of a Mr Q (no, really) from MI6 he practically sorted out the whole affair.

He is described by colleagues as 'formidable – a fiercely intelligent man', 'very black and white', and is 'very intolerant of fools and incompetents'. James, who is said to earn around £5,000 a day for his services, didn't mince his words when it came to the Dome. It probably didn't help that on the day he turned up to inspect his new patient, the assistant at the Dome box office offered him an OAP discount. 'I thought I looked about eighteen,' James joked. 'I work out in the gym every morning at 5.15 a.m. for an hour and a quarter. I'm in pretty good shape.' Certainly, he is pretty lean and mean. When asked why he decided to take on the impossible task of the Dome, James snapped back: 'Like Everest, it's there. You've got to climb it.'

Shortly after his appointment, James listed many flaws about the running of the Dome. He explained that because there was such strong political pressure to open on time, normal financial controls were disregarded. There were also, according to James, over 2,800 separate contracts in place, but no register of them was maintained. New liabilities kept appearing 'out of the woodwork'. There was also no register of the Dome's assets. He said that there were 'thousands of unresolved issues' over the physical assets and intellectual rights to the Dome's shows and contents, so they were not sure what they could and could not sell once the attraction closed. The original plans allocated £4 million for closure costs. James predicted that they could be as much as £28 million. He added that he thought it 'not perhaps a wise decision' to have built the Dome in the first place, certainly not at an isolated site with no parking facilities. Because of the uniquely confused situation at the Dome, it has been alleged that many companies or individuals took advantage for their own financial gain. But so far, only one company has been charged with conspiracy to defraud the NMEC.

Originally from Brighton, thirty-year-old Len O'Reilly had moved to London to try to get a job in the Dome. After working on the construction of the Dome's stage in September 1999, O'Reilly started work in the Dome's lighting department. In the meeting with David James, O'Reilly said that although he was incredibly enthusiastic at first, he was soon disillusioned by the amount of fraud, theft and bullying, which he claimed to have witnessed.

O'Reilly said that as soon as goods came into the Dome, invoices were destroyed and the goods moved out again. Once, he claims he saw someone loading up a boat which then crossed to the northern side of the Thames where its contents were loaded on to a van. O'Reilly recalled that on another occasion thirty black lights arrived at the Dome, but it was decided that they should have been silver. The cost for re-spraying was a staggering £37,800. The NMEC was then billed £6,000 for their transportation ... for a journey of 100 yards across the Dome. O'Reilly said that he carried them across 'in a golf buggy; the job took just hours, but later I discovered the Dome paid £6,000, which astounds me'. A spokesman for the Dome at the time said that moving such delicate items around the Dome can be quite costly.

O'Reilly was appalled, as were most of the staff, with the large amount of waste at the Dome. O'Reilly pointed out to James that unused Dome uniforms and tons of other stock were often thrown into skips: 'We had to literally throw out unused items, which was disgusting. Many contained things like brand-new staff uniforms and unused carpet tiles. Eventually, Dome officials told the staff to help themselves. Many of the staff employed at the Dome have a part of it in their homes, be it a table, chair or other souvenirs.'

Lighting technician Mike Shepherd was also shocked by the waste: 'Once we replaced £30,000 worth of light bulbs only to be told to replace them again by someone else who didn't know that they'd just been done. I tried to tell them but they said, "Just do it," so we did. It was the fault of the management, who were all too young and inexperienced, and the old-boy network that got relatives doing managerial jobs in various departments. A lot of things went missing: plasma-screen TVs worth £5,000 each were disappearing left, right and centre. Loads of brand-new stuff was thrown on to skips, which then vanished.'

Another worker, who did not want to be named, said: 'It seemed a real waste and in some cases things appeared to be disappearing into a black hole.'

One day in February 2000, O'Reilly was ordered to empty some filing cabinets and help sort through their contents. When he saw what one of the cabinet drawers contained, he stopped in amazement. They were full-colour architect's schematic drawings of the Dome's interior. He then came across the drawings of the De Beers vault, which showed how thick the walls were and so on. There were also documents that referred to heat- and light-sensitive security controls along with details of the power supply. 'It was basically a guide on how to access the area housing the diamonds,' said O'Reilly. 'This is a prime example of what a shambles the Dome is.'

O'Reilly was told that the contents of the cabinet should be placed in a rarely used office. He put the files at the bottom of the pile but one day noticed that they had been moved and placed in their own black folder. He expressed his concerns to a colleague called Richard Williamson, who was known as 'Barcode' (he got his nickname from a barcoding system he set up for Dome equipment), who told O'Reilly to take the blueprints home and keep them safe and not tell anyone for his own safety. He did this after discussing it with his mother and hid the plans on 25 April 2000 (he remembers that date because it was his mother's birthday), eventually forgetting about them.

Mike Shepherd's job included responsibility for every light bulb in the Dome: 'As lighting technicians, we had access to all areas of the Dome – wherever there was a light bulb, basically. Whether it was a 60-watt or 5,000-watt bulb, we were the ones who changed it.' This included the diamond vault. In the floor-to-ceiling glass cylinder that housed the Millennium Star, there were halogen spotlights at the top of the tube. The procedure was that in order to access the vault for maintenance work, De Beers had to be informed and a representative from De Beers had to be present along with someone from NMEC security. O'Reilly said: 'It was intended that the diamonds would not be accessible without a special De Beers key, but NMEC security were in fact able to access the vaults without it.' O'Reilly told James he knew of four occasions when technicians went in without a De Beers representative. It was commonly known in the lighting department that this was happening, but in the words of O'Reilly, 'Everybody wanted to keep their jobs.'

Late in April 2000, Shepherd climbed into the ceiling above the Millennium Star and lifted a hatch in order to access the halogen bulbs beneath it. It would take around thirty minutes to change the lights. Four feet beneath this tube, the Millennium Star gleamed proudly. As Shepherd put his hand below the hatch, he heard some rattling. Thinking that one of the tubes had come loose, he put his hand inside and to his surprise he pulled out a quartz copy of the Millennium Star. He threw it down to his colleague and they started playing catch with it in the area around the Money Zone. He discussed the find with his colleagues, including O'Reilly. They assumed it had been placed there by someone wanting to steal the Millennium Star. Mike Shepherd took the fake diamond home and stuck it on top of his computer.

O'Reilly tried reporting the incident to the police, but Greenwich CID apparently just laughed at him. He then did what any civilized worker would have done if they had found that someone had managed to access the diamond vault and was planning the theft of the millennium. He called Max Clifford. Max Clifford called the *Sunday Mirror*, and on 17 September 2000 a story that said O'Reilly had found plans to the De Beers vault went into the paper. Nothing was mentioned about the fake diamond.

Unsurprisingly, O'Reilly was sacked shortly after this story came out, but he managed to persuade the security team to give him a new pass as a 'consultant' so that he could still access the Dome whenever he liked. He added that: 'Security was so crap, people could move on and off the site all the time.' On 13 November 2000, six days after the attempted raid, he walked on to the site without showing his pass and delivered a copy of the *Sunday Mirror* article to Arnaud Palu, Gerbeau's right-hand man.

At the end of the 2001 meeting between David James and O'Reilly, James asked him what he wanted the NMEC to do about what he had told them. O'Reilly said he wasn't sure but thought that it was just time to come in and explain what had happened. David James thanked O'Reilly for the information before having him escorted off the premises.

It will probably never be known who, if anyone, was trying to steal the Millennium Star by gaining access to the vault and replacing it with a fake. Herr Droeschel adamantly said that he had no more orders for any more copies of the Millennium Collection. But such a story only makes one wonder how many more people thought that they could get away with stealing a diamond or two from the Dome?

'Brian' is a friend of an ex-cellmate of the Diamond Geezers. He is a professional, dangerous, armed robber – the real deal. Grey-haired Brian describes himself as a successful businessman. He looks the part: smart suit, Rolex (stolen, of course)], smart car (paid for in cash) and the latest mobile phone (even if he doesn't know how to check his voicemail or what his telephone number is and thinks that 3G is £3,000). Physically, he's a striking sight: 15 stone, hands the size of dustbin lids and size-13 feet shoehorned into a pair of Paul Smith shoes.

He is an old-style London gangster, where honour among thieves still means something. He would break his back for you if you needed his help, but by God you'd better do the same if he needed the favour repaid. Nowadays he says he's for the most part interested only in (legal) property development but could be persuaded to take part in some 'major scores' now and again. He is opinionated when it comes to evaluating the Diamond Geezers' attempt and provides some detailed expert criticism.

'Amateurs, bloody amateurs they were ... It was a wasted opportunity, diamonds on home soil and two half-arsed attempts. To me it was like watching England lose the World Cup final. They had the balls, didn't they? But fuck me they didn't have the brains. All right, the cops were on to them, but the plan was crap. Number one, you have more than one escape route, right? OK, so you're a professional robber, but other people ain't; you never know what's gonna go wrong. Meredith went to the wrong fucking pier, for Christ's sake! The river, yeah, that's a good route out, but you gotta have a back-up. I would have had three stolen vehicles parked at easy-to-reach locations, doors locked and keys under the seat, so they won't get nicked. If you need 'em, smash the window with one of these, right?'

Brian removes a bunch of keys from his pocket. Attached is a small 'punch-key', which was invented with the idea of smashing glass if a driver should end up in a river, trapped inside his vehicle.

'The trouble with this job is it's a very recognizable piece of merchandise. You're gonna have to either sit on it for a while or give it to someone who can. The only geezer who buys a rock like that is the Sultan of bloody Brunei.'

Brian is right. The Sultan of Brunei is rumoured to have smashed all records and bought the Centenary Diamond (at 273.85 carats, it's the world's third-largest diamond and is about the size of a tangerine) from De Beers, reportedly for £100 million in 2000. He certainly wouldn't want a dodgy diamond.

'You gotta cut it up, and even then it's not that easy. You don't just wander into the bloody [Hatton] Garden and say, "Chop this up for me and make it snappy." The boys were gonna hand it over to someone who had the know-how, someone who would've taken the stones off 'em for half a mil if they knew what they was doing. If they had got away with it, if I were a policeman I would've been knocking on diamond cutters' doors.

'Also, you shouldn't commit a robbery in your own bloody back yard. Risky. Most likely Old Bill knew where to look. London's full of fuckin' informers anyway. Do it in another town and the cops'll be hunting down the local mobs while you're safe at home in front of the telly.'

Brian says that a would-be thief would have no trouble finding out who would want to buy such 'hot rocks': 'If you want to get rid of fifteen rare budgerigars, I don't know a bird dealer but I know a man who does. If you want to offload a freight train of gold bullion in a hurry, I could put you in contact with someone whose aunt knows someone reliable. If you wanted your boss's car stolen and his kneecaps broken, I know some boys who'll do it for the craic – see what I mean? It's a tight-knit community, and someone, somewhere knows someone who can help.'

Ultimately, he thinks the Diamond Geezers' caution was their downfall. 'One of the problems with this lot was they was too bloody concerned with not gettin' done for robbery. In the end it was a waste of time – it don't matter what they should've got, it was the robbery of the millennium, so if you get caught, you're going down for a long fuckin' time.'

Brian is able to provide such detailed criticisms because, he claims, he had already thought about doing the job himself. 'Tell you what,' he said, 'I would've liked to have seen the missus' face when I brought that rock home.'

It seems as though there were hardly any South London criminals who had not thought about stealing the Millennium Collection.

'But,' Brian adds, 'the one thing you can't account for is a fuckin' grass. Must've been one. After all, the cozzers were waiting, weren't they? And they were all caught bang to rights. Makes me sick.'

Well, not quite all. Operation Magician wasn't entirely watertight, because one man did leak out.

17 – UNDERCOVERS, INFORMERS AND INSIDE MEN

'The whole "inside man" business is nonsense.'

DETECTIVE CHIEF SUPERINTENDENT JON SHATFORD

According to the plan described by Betson, the Diamond Geezers would arrive at the Mayflower pub's car park with the diamonds just after 10 a.m. to make the exchange. The Mayflower is an historical London pub; it's where the Pilgrim Fathers set off from in 1620 to colonize America, before they made a brief pit stop in Plymouth. The building dates from 1560, when it was called the Shippe. Some of the timbers from the pilgrims' ship, the *Mayflower*, were used in the rebuilding of the pub, and it's a great place at which to sit and admire the views across the Thames.

In fact one of the most striking views from the pub is of Wapping police station on the other side of the river. It's the home of the Thames Division, which was renamed the Marine Support Unit in 2001 and is part of an Operational Command Unit called Specialist Support, headed by a chief inspector. It has eighty-nine police officers and a fleet of twenty boats (fifteen patrol boats, one command vessel called the *Patrick Colquhoun* and four rigid inflatable boats). Officers from this station took part in Operation Magician. This, then, would seem to be a high-risk place at which to exchange the diamonds. If by some chance the police's intelligence was incorrect and the gang had struck on a different date or time, then knowing that the Mayflower pub was where the planned exchange would happen was obviously a bonus. It could be observed and approached by river from the comfort of Wapping police station, which meant that the police could still have got the Diamond Geezers with the goods as soon as they arrived.

Betson said that Tony told him that the meeting was to be at the Mayflower because it was on a quiet, dead-end street on the south side of the river, and meeting there had made sense to him because of this. He said he did not know about the police station. Betson also says, as do his friends and family, that the only reason Tony got away was because he was a police informer or undercover policeman, so the police let him go free.

Of course, the police maintain that Tony was not an informer or a policeman who set up an illegal sting operation. 'Clearly, he's not,' hurrumphed Shatford. 'They are saying that a policeman or a police informer was involved because it suits their case to say that. The whole "inside man" business is nonsense.'

So was Tony an informer or an undercover officer who entrapped the Diamond Geezers into a crime that they would not otherwise have committed? Or was he another Geezer who was simply lucky enough to get away?

There are some indications that there may have been an undercover police element. 'Attack, attack!' is a police code for the start of a raid. The command 'Attack, attack! Attack, attack!' was said by Betson to have been given by Tony. When 'Chainsaw Woody' Woodruff and 'Mad Dog' Hickson were arrested, you can hear quite clearly on the videotape a police officer saying: 'Attack, attack!'

'The Dome case looked like a stereotypical undercover operation,' said ex-undercover Scotland Yard detective and author of *The Filth*, Duncan McLaughlin. 'With the UC [undercover policeman] driving away through a cordon, that's just what would happen on cases I worked on.' Sometimes, elaborate set-ups are created that allow the undercover officer or informer to get away, or occasionally the UC is arrested with the suspects and later freed. Often, they might find themselves staring down the barrel of an armed policeman's gun, not knowing if the police know that they are on the same side. 'It's an unnerving experience, to say the least,' McLaughlin said.

Jon Shatford said that Tony, the white-van driver, simply drove away, and Sergeant Clive Drew said that 'efforts were made' to find him, but he 'slipped through the net'. Could the vast numbers of police simply have lost Tony in South-East London traffic? In the words of one criminal, 'A matchstick couldn't have got out of Greenwich that day without the police stopping it.'

'They think it's odd that the white van man managed to get away,' said Shatford, 'but if you put in context what actually happened on the morning, where we had the north side of the river to cover because we knew that there's someone there that we had to find. Then there's the whole scene at the Dome to cover as well, and I don't know which angle they're coming from, so I can't place officers all around in case they're spotted. I had to put all our eggs in one basket and concentrate our efforts around the vault because that's where the main agitators would be.'

Shatford is even prepared to admit that they were lucky to get Millman. 'I'd almost written off capturing Millman. I didn't know where Millman was going to be on the escape side on the north side of the Thames, so I'm very pleased we did. I'm surprised we didn't lose more, frankly.' In fact, it's highly unlikely that Tony was an undercover officer. Certainly, there is no concrete evidence in the Dome case that supports the theory. If there was, then surely the Flying Squad would have been better prepared on the day of the heist.

It seems that the white van did simply 'slip the net'. Visual contact was lost almost two and a half miles from the Dome in Anchor and Hope Lane. A surveillance officer stationed on top of Greenwich Hospital was the last one to spot it. Efforts were made, and a white van was stopped by a local unit, but it was unfortunately the wrong one. There would have to have been a pretty enormous police cordon to ensure his capture, and, as may be expected, Shatford was focused on the Dome. It is highly likely that the van driver was in fact simply one of the men working at Old Coal Yard dropping the Diamond

Geezers off. During the trial, the prosecution made efforts to identify the other man seen associating with Betson at Old Coal Yard, but to no avail. Eventually, on the judge's insistence, Betson named the man as 'Mickey Steele', which was taken to be a fabrication.

It is certainly a possibility, though, that the Flying Squad would have used an informer. Forty per cent of the Flying Squad's cases are solved thanks to information received. Generally speaking, informing is high-risk work with small reward. The payments received by informants are not as large as we, or they, might like to think. In 2000 the Flying Squad had a budget of £120,000 for the remuneration of informers. Each of the hundred registered informants on the Flying Squad's books makes an average of only £1,000 a year. There are occasional exceptions, but those who earn the larger rewards are so well connected that they are able to help police arrest dozens of criminals. One such example is the notorious armed robber and first 'supergrass', Bernie Smalls. In the 1970s Smalls made a fortune from grassing and reduced the numbers of armed robberies by 60 per cent before his ex-colleagues finally got wise. Another notorious informant was David Norris, a petty criminal who passed information about literally thousands of crimes during the 1980s. He was so prolific that many crooks attempted to use a 'Norris defence' to get themselves out of trouble, claiming in court that Norris had set them up. The use of this defence came to an abrupt halt in April 1991 when forty-nine-year-old Norris was shot dead outside his South London home. The only people that hardened criminals despise more than the police are child molesters and informers. Informers take their lives in their hands when they grass on their friends and colleagues.

Understandably, many police officers have strong reservations about collaborating with the enemy in the war against crime. The use of informers has also been associated with police corruption, dubious methods of recruitment, inadequate accountability and lack of supervision. Sometimes it even leads to criminal activity. Michael Michael (his real name) was one of Britain's most prolific drug runners, and when officers from Customs and Excise arrested him in 1998 they found £800,000 in cash and three tons of cannabis with an estimated street value of £11.6 million. Subsequently, drugs worth £49 million were recovered from a distribution network that is thought to have smuggled more than 110 kilograms of cocaine and 19,000 kilograms of cannabis into Britain. Customs officers were amazed to discover that Michael was already an informer for Scotland Yard. Questions were raised as to why he was allowed to continue operating such a huge drug-running network for several years, especially as the quality of information he had given police was not very high. Michael alleged that apart from information, he also gave a corrupt police officer up to £10,000 in cash to make sure he was left alone. The detective has not yet been charged but was suspended pending a disciplinary hearing.

The world of informing is a minefield for the police, and sometimes the criminal informer is able to take the authorities for a ride. Probably the most extreme example of this, and the example that the Flying Squad would most like to forget, is the 1995 case of a daring armed robber codenamed 'Selector' (he can't be named for legal reasons). The thirty-one-year-old West Indian man, already in jail for armed robbery, convinced detectives from the Flying Squad to release him from prison for two days so that he could take part in another armed robbery. The idea was that Selector would act as a participating informant, leading the detectives to a dangerous pair of robbers that they had been after for some time. They would catch them red-handed, making a lengthy conviction a certainty. In return, Selector would get a reduction in the time he had left to serve.

But Selector tricked the officers by sending them to the wrong location while he took part in the robbery of £1.5 million from a security van in South London. He even asked the Flying Squad officers to pick him up from his brother's house afterwards, persuading them that the time and location were changed at the last minute and he had been unable to let them know. He managed to hide a portion of his £200,000 cut. Shortly after the Flying Squad officers returned him to prison, Selector contacted the anti-corruption branch, CIB3, telling them that the officers were corrupt and had stolen the money. The officers, already professionally embarrassed, were put under intense scrutiny as a result.

Could Tony have been an informer? If the Diamond Geezers now believed that he was, why didn't they give the police more incriminating information about him? As one ex-commander of the Flying Squad, John O'Connor, said: 'Grassing a grass is fair dos.' One reason could be that the Diamond Geezers knew as much about Tony as you or I. In the criminal world of South London, you don't ask people's surnames. You only find them out if and when they get caught and their full name gets read out in court. Knowing as little as possible about your fellow criminal is reassuring if either of you ever gets arrested. There is a lot of trust involved in recommendation. You don't need any more information than a first name. Betson gave a description of Tony but claimed not to know any more for this reason. But it seemed unlikely that he wouldn't have been able to come up with anything more about him than a basic description if he really believed he was a grass.

Who else would grass on the Diamond Geezers? Records show that if there is an informer in a gang that commits a crime, it's usually the getaway driver. Meredith was the getaway driver. Meredith went to the wrong pier. Meredith blabbed as soon as he was caught while the others said nothing. And Meredith is perhaps not as respectable as he would have us believe. This was revealed during the trial when Heslop tried to correct one of Judge Coombe's mistakes. The following conversation took place in the absence of the jury:

Heslop: My Lord, may I deal with one matter which will relate to the direction to the jury on the facts? Dealing with the February robbery [the robbery attempt that took place in Nine Elms], which arose of course as a result of Mr Cherrill's [Meredith's solicitor] cross-examination—

Judge Coombe: Dealing with what?

MH: The February robbery, My Lord. The matter when the robbers escaped on a speedboat in the Thames, which was introduced during Mr Cherrill's cross-examination of Sergeant Drew. My Lord said that Mr Hurley had been arrested in relation to that. The evidence was that it was Mr Meredith who was arrested and interviewed.

JC: Forgive me. You may well be right. I do not actually think I said that Mr Hurley had been arrested in connection with that.

MH: The words you used were he had been arrested for a robbery in February, which was on a Securicor van and you made a reference to Mr Hurley.

JC: Yes.

MH: In fact, Mr Hurley was not arrested in relation to that, and the evidence shows that it was Mr Meredith who was arrested.

JC: Who brought that up?

MH: Mr Cherrill.

JC: I am sure if you say so, you are right. May I just go back to my note and see how I made that error? [Pause] Was it Sergeant Drew?

MH: Yes, My Lord, it was, and it was the cross-examination on behalf of Mr Meredith which dealt with the fact that following Meredith's interviews in relation to this case, he was interviewed in relation to another matter for which he was arrested, the February robbery.

JC: What I have is that he was also arrested on the occasion of a robbery in February. That is wrong, is it?

MH: My Lord, Hurley was not arrested. The evidence was that Meredith was arrested in relation to the February robbery.

JC: If anybody agrees with that, I have to confess it was a very long time ago, and if my note is defective I am sorry. Presumably he was interviewed?

MH: He was interviewed and he made no comment in the interview and he was released without charge.

JC: We all make mistakes, and I have been proved to have made one this morning.

This would indicate that there was much more to Meredith than he was letting on. Perhaps had the jury heard that Meredith had been arrested and questioned in connection with the Nine Elms Securicor robbery attempt in February 2000, then they may have found his duress argument even harder to believe, as well as, of course, his claim that he had no idea that he was participating in the attempted theft of the Millennium Collection.

So did the judge decide to inform the jury of his error that it was not Hurley who had been arrested in connection with the February robbery? He did not. In fact what Judge Coombe actually said in his summing-up was this:

'You do not have to judge Hurley, but he was observed, as you see from the schedule, with the speedboat on either side of 8 and 12 September, and then the officer could not say exactly when he left. It was borne out on behalf of one of the defendants that that man in any case had been arrested on another occasion for a robbery in February, which was a raid on a Securicor van, and people on that occasion, rather interestingly apparently, got away from the Securicor robbery on a boat on the Thames.'

What would the jury members be expected to make of this? They would draw the logical, if erroneous, conclusion that because James Hurley and Raymond Betson were friends (in Betson's words, they had known each other for twenty years), it would seem more likely that Betson was very closely linked to other armed robberies. This would mean that he was perhaps more likely to use violence than he was letting on in court.

Betson said that Meredith 'came recommended, and if someone came recommended then you took them on board. And Bill had met Meredith before and thought he would be OK for the job.' Recommended? Doesn't that suggest that someone from the criminal fraternity, in this case possibly Lee Wenham, knew that Meredith was a good man to have around when committing a crime?

If a criminal informer is arrested, his handler (police officer) will write to the judge asking that because of the help he has given he should be given a lighter sentence. Meredith got five years because he came in late and claimed that he did not know what the job was about. However, the argument against him being an informer is that if the rest of the Diamond Geezers thought he was one they would perhaps have dropped him in it at the trial, saying he was in on the plan.

As Meredith was questioned by police about the Nine Elms robbery attempt, it is possible that he exchanged freedom for information or the promise of future information. If Meredith was involved in the Nine Elms job, it is certainly conceivable that he could have heard about the Dome job from Wenham. But to inform on the Diamond Geezers and then to have become one of them at a later stage, knowing that he would have to suffer a lengthy public humiliation and serve a lengthy prison sentence, would have been stupid. The judge might have directed the jury to accept the duress argument in that case, too, on advice from Meredith's handler, whereas in actual fact he rubbished Meredith's defence. While Meredith may have been more dodgy than was let on in court, there is no evidence whatsoever to suggest that he would have informed on his criminal colleagues, and neither is there any evidence to say that Meredith was the getaway-boat driver at Nine Elms.

So much for undercover policemen and informers. But what about Betson's third conspiracy theory – inside men? Security guards have a long record of being tempted to rob the multimillion-pound cash loads they carry in their vans. Sometimes the sight of all that money, day in and day out, is too much, especially when the wage of a typical security guard doesn't come close to the national average. There aren't many perks, and, like informing, it is dangerous work for little reward. Brian Robinson and Mickey McAvoy relied on a security guard, Tony Black, for inside information when they raided Brinks Mat.

The Selector robbery described earlier also relied on a security guard to open the van and make sure that the cash was within easy reach. He was a better actor than Black, though, who soon succumbed under police interrogation. The apparently terrified security guard, Greg Hepburn, told his colleague and driver Mark Godfrey, 'They've got my mum!' before showing him a picture of his parents' home. He then lifted up his shirt, revealing a bomb strapped to his chest. He said that the gang had ambushed him on his way to work. Eventually, Selector 'grassed' on Hepburn and he was arrested.

There are also those who become security guards with criminal intentions from the start. The remarkable Selector managed to get a job with a certain well-known security company in the 1990s. He gave false references and the company failed to check if he had a criminal record. But again, in the case of the Dome, as far as the Diamond Geezers were concerned the poor security meant that there wasn't really a need for inside men. Shatford certainly didn't think that there was and made a very obvious point: 'Although we tried to be totally secret, I thought someone's got to notice something here. I thought there probably were inside men at the beginning, but if there were then they would have realized that we were there and that would have got back to the gang.' If there had been inside men, then they would have been watching the inside of the Dome carefully on the days of the earlier heist attempts and would have noticed a lot of suspicious activity. No security guards could be seen trying to guide in the JCB on 7 November. In addition, Shatford ordered the vault closed on days when he was unable to provide enough police cover to qualify as 'overwhelming force', and this in itself would raise the suspicions of a bent security guard.

But what about the other alleged inside man, Police Constable Michael Waring? This was a serious allegation for Betson to make and not only because Waring was a commended police officer with a blemish-free record. There are such things as crimes 'laid on', where an informer makes a suggestion to a criminal, makes a plan with them to commit a crime and then goes to the police, who arrange for an undercover officer. This is acceptable in the eyes of the law, but if a police officer instigates a crime, then it is quite another story. It can be argued that the police have overstepped the mark if they trap someone into a crime which would not otherwise have been committed.

Once detectives in Kent and London had established Betson's identity, a quick check of his police records soon revealed that Waring had actually already reported him to the Central Criminal Complaints Investigation Branch. His statement, which said that he suspected that Betson was involved in criminal activity, was recorded in a report made by a DS Wilkinson on 8 April 1998. The police decided to call Waring as a witness for the prosecution. Once they had decided that it was safe to mention Waring's name in relation to this piece of evidence in court, Betson was, according to his solicitor, 'completely shocked'.

During his cross-examination, Betson explained: 'I never intended to say Michael's name in court. So I told my solicitors about Tony but I said I'd been introduced to Tony by somebody I don't wish to mention, and that's why I didn't put his name in my defence statement. What made me change my mind about that is when the judge released this information and I realized that he [Waring] had been telling lies about me since 1998.'

In retaliation, much to Waring's horror, Betson named him as the man who, along with Tony, set up the crime. Then, to make matters worse, it emerged in the press that Waring, an amateur playwright, had been writing a screenplay called *Brothers in Law* about two brothers, one a policeman and one a criminal, who decide to commit a crime together. But the police and prosecution were happy for Betson to continue with these allegations, as there was no way a jury would take his word against Waring's unless some devastating evidence emerged. The police knew that there simply was none – Waring was 100 per cent straight. It also wasted the time and energy of the defence, whose limited resources would have been better spent trying to reduce the likelihood of a lengthy sentence by exposing flaws in the prosecution's case, such as the unreliability of witnesses coupled with the fact that Betson and his colleagues were not violent, professional, gun-toting robbers.

We have already heard Betson's story of how Michael Waring had approached him with the idea to leave the police force and commit a crime. Waring's version of events given during the trial is, as may be expected, rather different.

'Betson said he was a property developer,' said Waring. 'I didn't know if Ray had previous convictions, but I did believe that he made his living from crime. The first time I realized this was when he suggested that I should commit a crime with him. He made a criminal proposition to me, but not in relation to the Dome. The suggestions he made of acting together in crime were a lot earlier in our relationship.

'It is perfectly true that I may have experienced some frustration at the work I was doing for the police, some aspects of it, probably in his presence. A proposal was made, in the presence of my wife, that I should leave the police force, become a security guard and that Betson and some of his associates would rob the vehicle that I was supposed to be guarding. He suggested that I could be beaten up so that I could get out of the police force with an excuse. I felt threatened. He talked about armed robbery and the possibility of my being shot. I was concerned about the safety of my family. I played his conversation along, with the intention of bringing him down. I wanted to speak to Helen [his wife] first to find out what she thought.

'The conversation with Ray concluded with him saying that he would give me time to think about the offer. He then went to look for Susan [his partner] and left. Helen didn't want me to do anything to harm him because of the effect on Susan.

'I told Helen we had two options: either to go to the police and bring him down or to ignore him and tell him that I wasn't interested. Eventually, I chose the latter, and when we next saw him some months later I thanked him for trusting me and told him I wasn't interested. I added that the reason I was thanking him for his trust was because I could have gone along with the plan but reported it and brought him down. Ray replied that he wouldn't be very good at his job if he didn't know he could trust me.'

However, Waring eventually decided to go against the wishes of his wife. After hesitating for four months, he eventually went to the Central Criminal Complaints Investigation Branch to report Betson. In his statement, Waring said that he would help as far as he could in any investigation but was not prepared to give evidence or do anything that would lead to his family being at risk. However, the intelligence form which Waring filled out was never produced in court. Only a typed copy was shown; not even a photocopy of the original document. It did not mention that Betson had suggested committing an armed robbery. Betson's surname was incorrectly spelled and his date of birth was missing.

Interestingly, Waring said something slightly different later on in the trial. When talking about the alleged meeting during which the discussion about joining forces in an armed robbery was discussed, Waring said: 'He [Betson] ended by saying "You value your wife and children too much." I took this as an implicit threat and that if I did go to the police something would happen to them.' This statement has echoes of Meredith's claims, and this might reflect something that both men might have been advised to say to help emphasize the violent nature of the non-violent Diamond Geezers.

But under oath, the decorated policeman also said: 'I have never done anything to assist Betson criminally.' And there was no reason to suspect anything otherwise.

In fact, perhaps there would be more cause to suspect that Waring had actually been responsible for *hindering* Betson's criminal plans. Waring's wife, Helen, had trusted her husband not to grass on her sister's partner in 1998, but, of course, she did not know that her husband had betrayed this trust. Susan, Betson's partner, had visited the Dome along with her husband and Cockran on 1 September 2000. She knew what her husband was up to. The two sisters were close and often met to discuss the ins and outs of their relationships as well as their husbands' work. Any conversation between the two women about the Dome job could have got back to Waring, who may have overheard or been told by Helen, who mistakenly thought that her husband would put his family before his duty as a police officer.

In Shatford's words, the police first knew for certain that the Dome job was going to take place after Betson and Cockran were seen visiting the Dome together on 1 September. This was also the occasion when Betson's partner Susan went with them. Perhaps shortly after this, Waring was told by his wife or overheard her talking with her sister, and immediately reported this incident. It would seem, then, that Waring could have been the 'informer', if only to a limited extent because he was not in a position to know the details of the heist, as neither were the women, his source.

Whatever the case may be, Waring would like nothing more than to forget that the attempted heist ever happened. Shatford said: 'This whole episode has clearly had an impact on his home life, and he wants to just hide away, frankly. He had a situation where his wife's sister is obviously living with Betson. He knew Betson and had the dilemma of the policeman in the family. There's Betson who he's got bad feelings from during family occasions and then he's suddenly embroiled in the whole plot. He's been through some difficult times. He did report afterwards some of his concerns about his family when he heard he was going to be named.' It seems as though these 'concerns' were unfounded, however, as Waring has suffered no form of retribution, except maybe for a telling-off from his wife for disobeying her wishes.

So the informer/undercover operation angle was an invention of Betson's conspiracy-theory-led imagination. As Shatford said: 'What Betson has done is sat down and written a story for his defence, putting all these pieces together, which is what criminals do.' Betson made all the available pieces fit a story: the white van escaping; his policeman brother-in-law being 'in on the plan'; and, of course, the instigator, the mysterious Tony, who was never seen in the dozens of hours of video footage taken in the months leading up to the attempt.

Heslop: How many times did you meet Tony, apart from 6 October and 7 November?

Betson: Many times, many times.

MH: Can you give us an indication? Are we talking about daily or weekly or fortnightly or monthly?

RB: A couple of times a week, perhaps, sometimes.

MH: Where would you meet?

RB: I have met him down the farm, been down the farm with him, bit perhaps more than that – perhaps more than a couple of times a week; the Elephant and Castle, off the Old Kent Road, loads of places.

MH: Which farm?

RB: Tong.

MH: You have had access to all the video material in this case?

RB: Yes.

MH: Have you been able to see Tony captured on any of the video material at the farm?

RB: No, I haven't, no.

Surely the clinching argument that there was no police informer was the fact that the police knew surprisingly little about the heist. Shatford often used the words 'intelligence-led' policing to describe how the Flying Squad caught the Diamond Geezers. 'It's finding out that something is going to happen and putting measures in place to stop it happening,' he explained, 'trying to be one step ahead all the time.'

But he also said: 'I never knew how it was going to happen. I didn't know whether they would have inside agents, storm it with guns, how they would do it, no idea whatsoever. I knew they had a JCB, but what that was going to do I never knew until it went through the door on that morning.' This doesn't sound very 'intelligence-led'. In fact it sounds as though Shatford, despite five months of surveillance, was, for the most part, clueless as to how it would happen. Until the first attempt in October, the Flying Squad's favourite theory was that the Diamond Geezers would try to steal the diamonds while they were in transit, following in this way the modus operandi of the Aylesford and Nine Elms raids. Like these raids, this would require solid inside information and a carefully planned hijack, including tactics for preventing pursuit. While it would be unwise to discount completely the chance that the Flying Squad may have got one or two snippets from the odd informer, they certainly didn't find out anything that they weren't able to get from their own observations.

But Betson was not the only one using the white van to try to 'write a story' for his own benefit – the police weren't much better. A puzzling part of the equation for Shatford is that the Diamond Geezers, against the standard advice of any professional thief such as Brian, didn't carry guns. 'Well, all my intelligence was that they were going to be heavily armed,' said Shatford. 'I don't know what it was. I do think that they had guns thereabouts that we didn't recover, and for whatever reason they decided not to carry them in there on that day. I speculate that the guns could have been left in the white van that got away. My own theory was that their guns were in there.'

The reason for Betson's convoluted inventions is partly professional embarrassment on his part (he has confessed that he doesn't know how they could have been caught, and refuses to accept the simple fact that the Diamond Geezers were spotted, observed, followed and captured), coupled with the desire to draw some of the blame away from the gang. There was, of course, one more, very important reason to lie: to protect those who were really responsible for organizing the job.

18 – MR BIG AND THE BUYER

'Piss or get off the pot.'

RUSSIAN DEPUTY FINANCE MINISTER VALERY RUDAKOV, LOSING HIS TEMPER WITH DE BEERS

To get to the bottom of the mystery as to who exactly was the mastermind behind the plan to steal the Millennium Collection, and who was going to buy it, it is necessary to take a trip to Marbella.

Marbella forms part of the infamous Costa del Crime, the Spanish coastal resort area to which many of Britain's most notorious criminals flee when the heat gets too much at home. Scotland Yard reported that there are 35 outstanding extradition requests and estimated that there are more than 230 known British criminals in Marbella who would be arrested on sight if they were to set foot again in the UK. Because there are so many British criminals in Marbella, Scotland Yard has been sending specially trained multilingual officers over to work with Unidades de Drogas y Crimen Organizado (UDYCO), formed by the Spanish police in 1997 to fight organized crime. They are sometimes referred to as 'Marbella Vice', and Marbella is now known as 'the European Miami' because drug lords from all over the world have set up homes there, from which they run their empires.

Famous Brit crims now in Marbella include Pat Adams, the oldest of the notorious Adams brothers, who fled the UK to escape the attention of MI5. He's now taking care of the family's interests abroad, which are thought to include supplying drugs to clubbers. Also in Marbella is Mark Murray, the man in charge of dealing at the club where the pill which killed Leah Betts was bought; Clifford Saxe, believed to be the mastermind behind the £6 million Security Express robbery; Mickey Green, also known as 'the Pimpernel', a multimillionaire criminal who has been on the run for more than twenty years and is believed to be one of the most senior figures in the British underworld. Marbella was also home to Michael McGuinness, murdered in August 2000, who was known to have been working with traffickers linked to the gang that murdered Dublin journalist Veronica Guerin.

Marbella is undisputedly the 'quality resort' of the Costa del Sol, where restaurants and bars are stylish and everything costs considerably more than in other towns. It has the highest per-capita income in Europe and more Rolls-Royces than any European city apart from London (although many of the classy cars here have been stolen elsewhere and re-registered in Spain). The truly rich don't stay in Marbella itself. They secrete themselves away in villas in the surrounding hills or lie around on phenomenally large and luxurious yachts at the marina and casino complex of Puerto Banús, almost four miles out of town towards San Pedro, where James Hurley, the Diamond Geezers' original getaway boatman, has a villa.

With all this wealth swimming about, Marbella has attracted a vicious new breed of criminal who uses violence to steal other gangs' drugs. Some have even used torture to extract information from rivals. In 2001 seven people were killed in eight days of street shootings in Marbella as war broke out between local and Colombian drug dealers. The year before, in one three-month period, eight suspected drug traffickers were murdered. The latest and most lethal addition to the Costa's crime cocktail are the Russians. Shatford isn't sure what would have happened to the diamonds if they had been stolen by Betson and co., but when pushed he makes a hesitant guess: 'Well, I don't know. All sorts of things have been suggested. One of them was the Russian Mafia, which had some weight ... They certainly wouldn't go through all that trouble unless someone was lined up.' It's dangerous to speak Russian in Marbella, as one branch of the very active Russian Mafia make a living from kidnapping their rich countrymen for ransom. Of course, the Russians have not limited themselves to drugs and kidnapping; diamond smuggling is also rife.

One of the many powerful figures seen in Marbella was Vladimir Putin, who made frequent visits to Russian media mogul Boris Berezovsky's villa in Marbella, slipping in discreetly and without a visa. Putin, now the Russian premier, was Presidential Security Council Chief at the time. The purpose of the trips was to plot with Berezovsky, who controls Russia's main national television network, how to take over from Boris Yeltsin. Five visits occurred in the summer of 1999 and in 2000, a few months before he took power in 2001. Putin's visits were discovered accidentally by Spanish police who were spying on a suspected Russian Mafia boss in the house next door. His name was Semyon Yukovich Mogilevich.

Ukrainian-born Mogilevich has been described by the CIA as 'the most dangerous mobster in the world'. A 1995 classified FBI report stated that Mogilevich was the head of the 'Rising Sun', a global crime organization, although he has never been convicted of a crime. Until 1988 Mogilevich had limited himself to running his empire in Russia, but he made a powerful friend in the shape of the late media tycoon Robert Maxwell. Maxwell pulled some strings and got Mogilevich and twenty-three of his henchmen bona fide Israeli passports. This enabled Mogilevich to keep an eye on his $40 billion money-laundering racket, which ran from the Middle East to London. Maxwell helped set up bogus companies through which illegal money could be laundered and received a healthy percentage in return. Mogilevich has travelled all over Europe, putting his fingers in all sorts of pies, most worryingly becoming involved with international terrorists. Associates of Osama bin Laden met Mogilevich in Marbella in 2000. French and British Special Services reported that Mogilevich had sold radioactive materials to a company belonging to bin Laden. Members of bin Laden's al-Qa'eda network were later arrested in Paris and found to be carrying U-235 (a radioactive material used in nuclear weapons) in a suitcase. Mogilevich also sold the secret American-designed spy software PROMIS (Prosecutor's Management Information Systems) to bin Laden for £3 million. This remarkable piece of software enabled bin Laden to spy on the USA and Britain in the 1990s and monitor their efforts to track him down, as well as providing him with the safest routes through which to launder money. In fact much of al-Qa'eda's money was rinsed through Sierra Leone in exchange for diamonds. Mogilevich is also wanted by the FBI for laundering $10 billion made from the sales of stolen art, gems and Afghani-produced narcotics.

Mogilevich says he has been unfairly targeted by investigators because he's a convenient target who looks the part. 'I am big. I catch the eye,' he said. 'I am a businessman.'

On hearing this quote, a senior US official retorted dryly: 'If his business includes contract killings, extortion, fraud, money laundering, drug trafficking and prostitution, then he is a businessman.'

One of Mogilevich's 'businesses' included involvement in the illicit trade in Russian diamonds. Russia is the world's second-largest producer of diamonds, and because of the endemic corruption, particularly among the government, millions of carats of diamonds are smuggled on to the black market each year. In fact diamond smuggling is almost encouraged by the authorities. The reason for this is that the Russian government would support anything that caused De Beers trouble. To say that there is absolutely no love lost between De Beers and Russia is putting it mildly.

In a secret deal struck during the Cold War, De Beers negotiated with Russia to buy all the diamonds that Alrosa, their government-owned diamond production company, produced (at a bargain-basement price) to stop the market becoming flooded. Unfortunately for De Beers, they underestimated the amount that Russia could supply and were overwhelmed with millions of ¼-carat diamonds. As a result, De Beers launched an advertising campaign that focused attention on the cut, quality and colour of a diamond. Suddenly size wasn't important. The stock was sold. The average size of a diamond sold fell from 1-carat in 1939 to ¼-carat by 1970. But much to De Beers' dismay, Russia kept increasing diamond production.

In addition, enterprising Russians had now started to smuggle gem-quality diamonds out of the country disguised as industrial diamonds, rather than selling them to De Beers for a fraction of what they were worth. Part of the reason for this was that the Russian *nouveau riche* were trying to hide some of their new-found wealth abroad. De Beers were unable to stop millions of carats of Russian diamonds finding their way on to the markets and thereby devaluing the precious stone.

By May 2000 relations between De Beers and Russia had fallen to an all-time low. Already angry that De Beers had been buying their diamonds for a fraction of their worth for several decades, a new deal struck in 1998 had actually made things worse for the Russians. Finally, in early 2000 Deputy Minister of Finance Valery Rudakov, who heads the Russian government's diamond and precious metals agency, snapped and told De Beers to 'get out of Russia'.

Rudakov believed that De Beers had taken advantage of Alrosa in a deal that had guaranteed sales of at least $550 million to De Beers. But as long as Russia needed the money, De Beers got the diamonds. And Russia really needed the money. In fact Russian Prime Minister Yevgeny Primakov had approached De Beers early in 2000 to discuss a loan backed by diamonds. Although Alrosa is the world's second-largest producer of diamonds, the De Beers cartel has ensured that Russia, like Africa, has not profited from its natural wealth. In 1999 Alrosa produced $1.5 billion worth of diamonds (£820 million) but made a loss of 3.7 billion roubles (£100 million). The reason for this, apart from the bargain-basement selling price, is that Alrosa's diamond production costs are five times as high as De Beers'.

Rudakov's next argument with De Beers focused on the Lomonsov diamond field. De Beers had invested £30 million in a 27 per cent share in the diamond field that is one day expected to yield £12 billion of diamonds. De Beers were not anxious to flood the market with yet more Russian diamonds, so stalled development for several years, until Rudakov's patience snapped and he told them to 'piss or get off the pot' in May 2000. De Beers took his advice and pulled out, leaving the Russians high and dry after ten years of making investment plans from the expected future profits. Alrosa has been left unable to manage the mine profitably.

As a result, smuggling is the natural course to take for any Russian who manages to extract some diamonds from the Russian mines. Diamond smuggling is carried out by anyone, from villagers to organized-crime gangs to senior government ministers, including Yevgeny Bychkov, the former head of the government's gem and precious metals agency. Bychkov was charged in 2000 with smuggling $183 million (£100 million) worth of diamonds and gold out of Russia to a company based in San Francisco. Russia's notoriously weak and corrupt law-enforcement officials are powerless to stop the thousands of diamond smugglers whose networks have become so effective that they are used to smuggle illegal diamonds from all over the world. Of all the countries in the world, Russia was the only place where the stolen De Beers Millennium Collection would attract serious criminal interest from expert smugglers, who could use their international networks to cut and resell the diamonds on the black market unnoticed and at a substantial profit.

The man who was going to take the De Beers Millennium Collection off the Diamond Geezers' hands was one of Semyon Mogilevich's lieutenants, a gem smuggler by the name of Alexei Vlasov. Based in Marbella, Vlasov was a diamond smuggler *par excellence*, with a network that stretched across Russia, the Middle East and Europe. Vlasov's smuggling operation would typically run like this. In Moscow he would go to a hotel and meet the manager, who was his contact. The cut diamonds were brought to him in a luxury suite where they were carefully inspected. They were then packed in a soda can with a false bottom, or in sandwiches, toys or false-bottomed suitcases. Vlasov would then fly to Turkey, using an Israeli passport, and from there to Belgium. Customs officials were paid off or fooled by Vlasov's paperwork. Thanks to the bribing of senior government officials, Vlasov was sometimes able to get his hands on the best forgeries of official papers in all of Russia, which allowed him to take gems in and out of the country safely.

Vlasov eventually delivered the diamonds to a large, well-known, seemingly legitimate diamond firm in Antwerp. Police estimate that Vlasov made about thirty smuggling runs to Antwerp along a variety of routes in five years. Stones were smuggled into Belgium in two ways: smaller hauls by aeroplane, larger quantities by boat, which travel via Marbella before the gems are collected by local couriers and transported either by boat, lorry or car (variety helps throw the police off the scent) to their final destination. These larger shipments contained between 200 and 500 stones. Sometimes they were hidden in a cargo of cotton thread. Again, the boxes weren't opened at Customs thanks to a few well-placed bribes. Once Vlasov got the diamonds to Antwerp, the money flowed back to the Russian Mafia.

Sometimes, lured by the high prices for superior-quality stones from Africa, Vlasov collected uncut diamonds from Sierra Leone. Typically, Russian diamonds are of poor quality when compared with African diamonds and sell for a lot less. This is why Vlasov would sometimes be tempted to take his chances with the rebel warriors of Liberia and Sierra Leone, where gems of the highest quality can be found. The Sierra Leoneans are not interested in cash, however; they want weapons. So instead of taking money to Sierra Leone, Vlasov paid an arms dealer (his source was based in Bulgaria), who then shipped weapons direct to Sierra Leone. Diamonds from Sierra Leone also arrived in Marbella by boat for European distribution. In Antwerp's diamond-cutting shops, these rough diamonds were sliced and burnished into finished gems before being sold to a dealer, who mixed them with legitimate diamonds, and they vanished into the legal trade. This is how conflict and stolen diamonds, an estimated 10 per cent of the business, taint the stream.

Vlasov was unable to resist the proposition put to him by the Diamond Geezers. It's not known what was said, or exactly what arrangements were made, but to make it worth their while, Vlasov would have had to have bought the stolen De Beers Millennium Collection for at least £1 million. And this would be a very good deal. The 203-carat Millennium Star could be cut into a variety of internally flawless D-coloured (the most expensive kind) 1- to 3-carat stones, as could the much sought-after blue stones. Altogether, once cut into smaller stones, the twelve diamonds would be worth at least £2.5 million on the black market, so Vlasov was confident that he could expect easily to more than double his money for the entire collection once it was cut up and distributed among his extensive smuggling network.

The Diamond Geezers had strong connections with Marbella, where Vlasov had used Mogilevech's influence to help set up his European base. James Hurley had a villa there. The *Daily Telegraph* and the Spanish paper *El Mundo* described Hurley as the alleged 'mastermind' of the Dome caper. The police observed Hurley associating with many internationally successful criminals in Marbella and believed that he fulfilled some of the roles that Betson said were performed by the mysterious 'Tony'. He had strong connections with the building trade in South London, some of whom worked in and around the Millennium Dome. But Hurley was no criminal mastermind. He may have helped with some of the legwork for Betson, his friend of twenty years, such as getting hold of Dome uniforms, blueprints, mobile phones and other equipment for the Diamond Geezers – and he was even mentioned on Vlasov's Interpol 'red notice' (a detailed report of a suspected criminal's activities) as an 'accomplice' – but he was not the instigator. The mastermind who provided the brains, the contacts and the finances for the raid is one step further up the criminal ladder. A number of rumours circulated at the time as to who 'Mr Big' was, but the most likely candidate by far is another middle-aged South Londoner who was linked to the Dome job in a number of ways.

He cannot be named here for legal reasons, but for the purposes of this book he will be known as Jack Carter. Carter is not much to look at. He is of medium build, with short, close-cropped straight brown hair, but he is one of the most feared gangsters in Britain. He has had some phenomenally successful criminal ventures, but, like the best criminals across the globe, little is known about his past and he has a very short criminal record. Mention Jack Carter's real name in the criminal world of South-East London and you are met with a stone wall of silence. Carter is a psychopath with a ruthlessness matched by almost no other criminal operating in the UK today. He is the embodiment of the expression 'mad, bad and dangerous to know'. 'He bumps people off who he thinks *might* be informers,' said one nervous former associate. 'He doesn't know for sure, but just to be on the safe side he bumps 'em off anyway.' This made it hard for any law-enforcement agency to get close to any of his tightly run operations.

Carter is believed to have been behind an international drugs-smuggling network, which involved the transportation of cocaine from South America to Britain by boat. In the first operation of its kind, Customs tracked the boat with the help of the Royal Navy and the Royal Air Force. From above, the boat carrying the cocaine was watched by an RAF Nimrod, originally designed as a maritime patrol and anti-submarine aircraft, and less well known for its secondary role in counter-drugs operations. For this purpose, the original maritime equipment was removed from the aircraft and replaced with a highly sophisticated and sensitive suite of systems used for reconnaissance and the gathering of electronic intelligence by an eight-man crew. There is an RAF Nimrod, never formally acknowledged, based in Puerto Rico, and another at an American air-force base in Florida.

From below, the boat was being tracked by one of Britain's four HMS *Vanguard* nuclear submarines, carrying 16 infamous Trident missiles and 146 men. Capable of circumnavigating the globe without surfacing, HMS *Vanguard* had been checking her Y2K compliance until orders were received for this unusual mission – her first test of tracking drugs smugglers. Again, this role would never be officially acknowledged.

And although the operation was considered a success after the boat's crew were arrested and successfully prosecuted, Customs were unable to gather enough evidence to prosecute Carter. Carter has since looked for other means of investing his millions and has moved away from the lucrative world of drug smuggling, partly because the risks of a lengthy prison sentence and/or assassination are so high. There are several international criminal gangs that would happily kill anyone for a variety of reasons. Privately, police believe that Carter financed the Diamond Geezers' operation and that he was part of a growing trend of 'old-school' blaggers who had tired of the risks associated with drug dealing and had reverted to good old-fashioned smash-and-grab robberies.

Typically, since the 1980s many aspiring South London criminals have tried to battle their way up the criminal ladder by starting with armed robbery. The root of South London crime is in poverty and the need to escape it. When former Conservative Party chairman Lord Tebbit said 'Get on your bike', the poor of South London were listening. In the early 1980s, armed robbery rocketed to out-of-control levels as these ruthless capitalists turned South London into the Wild West in their search for a stake. Most robbers fail to advance up the criminal ladder simply because it takes someone with exceptional talent to escape being caught.

Some are marked for distinction by having 'more front than Brighton beach', as well as brains, originality and good luck: for example, the robber who pretended to be blind, carrying a white stick and wearing sunglasses, and surprised the security-van courier, or the robber who used a wheelchair to rob a supermarket, concealing a shotgun under a blanket spread across his lap. Another made an appointment with a bank manager to discuss the possibility of a loan before producing a handgun, arranging a completely different type of withdrawal. More often than not things go wrong, like counter staff disappearing from view, or the thieves arriving a few minutes after the tills have been cleared. There are numerous tales of cases where the police were already present when the gang arrived to carry out a robbery, and a further two cases where robbers accidentally rammed police cars during the getaway; spotting the police caused panic in the wheelman.

The next step for the criminal high-flier is to invest in the drugs trade. 'Yeah, most money, particularly where I come from in South London, got illegally from armed robberies will end up reinvested in some sort of drugs deal,' said one jailed armed robber. 'If you want to turn some money over and get a good profit, the only obvious thing nowadays is drugs.'

Drugs gangs transformed the South London crime scene. One older robber said with some sense of nostalgia that the greater number of armed robbers involved in drugs dealing had made people more suspicious of each other, and that rather than just spending the money on going out and having a good time, it was continually being reinvested: 'People aren't so sociable. They're more paranoid, you know, and whereas you used to have big family get-togethers, they don't happen any more. Everyone is suspicious and wary with this drugs business.' Serious dealers need armed protection from rivals and double-crossers, grasses may need to be eliminated, perhaps bent coppers need to be bought to limit the interest from police, and after arrest a crash course in evading the due process of the legal system is needed from the best solicitors money can buy. Those at the top of their game, the 'core nominals', as the police describe them, are adept at multitasking, and are able to make life-changing decisions frequently and within seconds while keeping their dealings from the police (who can make as many mistakes as they like, whereas a core nominal can't afford to make one).

Armed robbery diminished in the 1990s because of improvements in security and the ease with which it is now possible to start drug dealing. But now it is on the rise again. The reason is that many successful dealers, now in middle age, are fast approaching 'burnout' with the stress of running a drugs empire and the influx of ruthless foreign gangs that globalization has brought to the UK. They are being tempted to revert to the days of the simple stick-up. The reasoning of the old guard is perfectly rational. In the UK in 2000 there were fifty-two murders linked to organized crime — thirty-three of them were committed in South-East London, and the majority of those were drug-related. 'It's a whole new bloody ball game,' says Brian, the former armed robber we met in Chapter 16. 'The drugs gangs are turning over millions in a very fucking competitive market. To be able to hold on to it, you've gotta be prepared to bump a few people off, whether they're grasses or rivals. Some get carried away, get paranoid and start bumping off lads for no good reason, just 'cause they think there's a chance of them informing. The older lads are sick of it and long for the good old days where you took the money, divvied it up and went on your way.'

One senior detective in the Met agreed: 'The drugs underworld is a dangerous place to operate. We're getting an average of probably one hit-man killing a month in London and the Home Counties at the moment, and some of the old gangsters are losing their bottle. They're getting nostalgic for the good old days when they'd put up the cash for a team to rob a security van of a couple of hundred grand. Everyone gets their share and that would be the end of it.'

It's becoming a popular move among South London's criminal elite. In 2000 the number of armed robberies on goods in transit rose by 19 per cent. The sophisticated security methods which had contributed to the decline in these robberies in the 1990s has now been matched by the much improved tactics and weaponry, thanks in part to the massive increase in demand for guns combined with the crooks' many years of experience. And instead of taking the risk themselves, core nominals are in the position of being able to finance daring raids thanks to a network of criminal hopefuls who come to them with a variety of plans for attacks on vans and warehouses. Gangs are formed containing a mixture of young 'intermediate diversifiers' such as Betson and Ciarrocchi, who are keen to raise a stake for whatever reason, as well as 'old lags', career robbers who are not blessed with the success of people like Carter and are still looking for that big score. These gangs of semi-professional blaggers are capable of mounting 'one-hit wonders' on everything from airport warehouses to multimillion-pound cash deliveries by security vans. The risk is theirs and theirs alone; someone like Carter would never take part in the actual crime. The gang would do the job for a prearranged fee and Carter would pocket the rest.

They are always on the lookout for new 'soft' targets that don't have the level of sophisticated protection of most high-street banks. For example, some gangs are switching from hijacking security vans carrying cash to trucks transporting millions of pounds' worth of computer chips because they are nowhere near as well secured. Organized criminals are believed to be shipping many of the stolen computer chips to the Far East and Eastern Europe, where they are used in pirated hardware as part of a thriving black market. The components are easy to smuggle – a suitcase could hold £2 million worth of chips. Other stolen goods are being sold via bogus companies on the Internet and are then 'legally' traded in a carousel fraud, a complex crime that requires a sophisticated and intelligent criminal network to pull it off. This is the crime for which Carter was eventually prosecuted. The scam occurs when stolen computer chips are smuggled out of the country and are then imported VAT-free from elsewhere in the European Union back into the UK. They are sold on to an end purchaser, who pays VAT and claims it back from the government. But the original importer, who should now be paying the VAT received on the deal, has disappeared, giving the con its other name – 'missing trader' fraud – and the goods are then sold back to an innocent party on the Continent. So they are getting the full market price for their computer chips and a healthy VAT rebate from the government. Carousel fraud is reckoned to cost the government an astounding £7 billion in lost VAT each year. Carter's golden touch deserted him when, in an eighteen-month joint operation by HM Customs and Excise and the National Crime Squad, he was arrested for organizing a complex multimillion-pound VAT fraud involving the illegal importation and exportation of computer chips. It was thought that the chips were stolen, but this allegation was never proved in court. The operation began in April 2000 when an associate of Carter's was observed setting up a bogus company in South-West London. After several attempts, Customs managed to bug Carter's car, and he was heard discussing his plans in a motorway petrol station. Carter was arrested and convicted in 2001. He was sentenced to four years and fined £3 million. Very little information has been released about Carter, and none of the officers involved in his case wants to talk about him because, they say, nearly all of them received death threats throughout the trial. Officers also reported that associates of Carter's were even recorded discussing whether to 'bump off' the trial judge.

At Heathrow airport, there is around one major heist a week. Usually, the thieves are after computer chips stored in poorly protected warehouses or delivery vans. In December 2003 robbers drilled through a wall in a cargo area at Heathrow and stole computer chips worth £3.5 million. The chips had just arrived on a Korean Air jet and were scheduled for delivery to the computer firm Samsung. In January 2004 thieves made off with computer chips believed to be worth more than £4.6 million after a driver left his van unattended. In February 2004 £1.75 million in cash was taken during a raid from a cargo area at the Menzies World Cargo warehouse. On 26 March 2004 a high-value load of electronic equipment was delivered to a warehouse in London by DHL. Shortly after delivery, the warehouse received a telephone call from a man claiming to be from DHL. He stated that there had been a fault with the shipment and quoted the house waybill number. The bogus driver then arrived at the London premises and collected the goods. In April 2004 a warehouse worker went AWOL with a box of computer chips worth £1 million.

Then, in May 2004, police officers managed to prevent what would have been Britain's largest robbery since Brinks Mat when an eight-man gang tried to steal £80 million in gold and cash from a Swissport warehouse at Heathrow. Unfortunately for the would-be thieves, as with the Diamond Geezers, armed officers were lying in wait to nab them in the act. There are many striking similarities between the Dome and Swissport gangs. The majority of both were relatively unknown to the police and did not have any history of violent or serious crime; both raids incorporated a ramming vehicle, and both were exceptionally audacious and ambitious.

This spate of robberies at Heathrow prompted the Metropolitan Police to set up Operation Grafton, which had, until May 2004, remained 'conspicuously inconspicuous', according to Detective Inspector Paul Douglas, the head of its intelligence section. The unit, officially made public in the summer of 2004, was set up in response to an incredible increase in raids committed by organized gangs at Heathrow which rose 21 per cent in 2003, with a total of fifty-seven raids and thefts netting criminals £25.3 million, almost ten times the amount of money robbed from banks and building societies for the same period in the whole of the London area. According to Detective Inspector Douglas, warehouses are becoming more popular targets than banks and building societies, which have superior protection and alarm systems. As a result, the old-fashioned and clumsy high-street smash-and-grab raid has gone out of fashion, but warehouse raids and carefully planned hijacks are on the up. Operation Grafton relies heavily on its intelligence section to gather information covertly about possible robberies before passing them on to proactive agencies such as the Flying Squad.

Police officers believe that information is often leaked by poorly paid warehouse staff (Swissport staff went on strike in 2003 in a dispute over pay) on a regular basis in return for cash rewards from criminal gangs. For example, the Swissport gang had papers on them which allowed them to pass security on the front gate.

The police are naturally concerned at the increase in these 'one-hit wonders', and the Flying Squad are unable to cope despite the occasional conspicuous success such as the arrest of the Diamond Geezers and the Swissport gang. The problem is that so many crimes are being committed by people who aren't 'faces', who aren't familiar to the Flying Squad, that investigations take so much longer, and even if they manage to nab the criminals in the act the 'Mr Bigs' almost always get away, even if the police have a pretty good idea who orchestrated the raid. And an important source of information for the Flying Squad has been drying up in recent years. The squad have relied on dozens of grasses and informants for over forty years, but they are now becoming an endangered species as the huge amount of money involved in drug dealing has made life cheap and they are very likely to be eliminated for their trouble. The Met estimate that there are twenty active assassins currently residing in the South London area, and there are known to be twenty contracts out. This is bad news for the Flying Squad, who have traditionally solved about 40 per cent of their investigations thanks to information provided by grasses.

The Met has a dirty-dozen list of top villains it believes are financing these teams of robbers to carry out their orders. Carter is one of these 'dirty dozen', and he has been linked to the Dome job in a variety of ways. Associates of Carter's are providing support to the families of the Diamond Geezers while they are in prison. Another clue comes from the equipment that Ciarrocchi was using to track police frequencies. This equipment is not easy to get hold of. According to Duncan McLaughlin, the Flying Squad radios, which were brand new in 2000, randomly jump through a hundred frequencies per second, making conversations impossible to track – or so it was thought. When police raided Carter's home, they found some of the most sophisticated counter-espionage equipment available in the world today. This included an Optoelectronics Communications Interceptor and a Hewlett-Packard 8594E Spectrum Analyser worth almost £15,000, as well as a device used for the tracking of vehicles and a list of radio frequencies used by government agencies, from the ambulance service to the Flying Squad. Also found were two very powerful communications receivers, an ICOM IC-R7000 and an ICOM IC-R10 and aerial. These devices were supplied by perhaps the most useful man in any criminal's address book. Known simply as 'the Bug', this man (who also cannot be named for legal reasons) supplied the discerning criminal with a variety of the most sophisticated and most expensive counter-espionage equipment on the market today, and has a knack of being able to get information from the most hard-to-get places. Perhaps even more remarkably, the police also found in a kitchen drawer the top-secret order given by Customs authorizing the opening of Carter's mail. Only the local postmaster and a senior investigating officer from Customs are supposed to see such an order. The postmaster is supposed to collect the target's mail personally without informing any of his colleagues.

In the Diamond Geezers' case, Ciarrocchi had a photocopy of the list of radio frequencies, and an ICOM IC-R10 and an Optoelectronics Communications Interceptor were found in the van after the gang were arrested. A sophisticated transceiver was recovered from Meredith's boat. One of the most interesting finds to come from the arrest of Carter was his address book. This little black book contains only a few names, but it includes the phone numbers of Lee Wenham, James Hurley, Aldo Ciarrocchi and Ray Betson, names that meant nothing to the Customs officers at the time of his arrest, and so their significance went unnoticed.

On 24 July 2001 Vlasov was caught smuggling fourteen consignments of diamonds totalling more than $2.75 million (£1.5 million) in an operation involving the Russian police and the CIA. Vlasov was also charged with thirteen black-market diamond purchase and sale deals amounting to over $2.5 million (£1.4 million). The CIA and the Russian police had waited until they had a watertight case and the best opportunity to arrest Vlasov and as many of his cronies as possible. Vlasov is now serving a dozen years in a Russian jail.

With the Diamond Geezers safely locked up, and the CIA watching Vlasov, who had moved his operations back to Russia, the Flying Squad headed to Marbella. On a May morning in 2001 James Hurley drove into the centre of Puerto Banús, where he would normally have lunch. Two Flying Squad detectives were watching his every move from an unmarked car, a vanload of UDYCO offices ready to back them up. As Hurley locked his car, the detectives put on the baseball caps that identified them as police officers, threw open the doors and ran towards the shocked Hurley, brandishing handguns and shouting at him to get down on the ground. He was handcuffed and was having his rights read before the UDYCO officers had even got out of their van.

'He [Hurley] is currently being held in custody. We are asking for his extradition,' said an officer at the time. 'It is a matter that will be before the Spanish courts, and they will decide if his extradition will be granted.' It was hoped that a new extradition treaty signed with Spain in March 2001 would mean that he would be back in Britain quite quickly, but after nine months waiting in a Spanish prison Hurley was freed at a hearing at the Madrid High Court on 27

February 2002. British prosecutors told the tribunal that even though police were able to link Hurley to the crime through surveillance film, showing him testing the boat with Millman, Lee Wenham and Cockran on several occasions in September 2000, they were not 100 per cent sure of securing a conviction and were therefore unable to convince the Spanish courts that Hurley should be extradited. Hurley is the most fortunate member of the Diamond Geezers. While his friends are cooling their heels in 6-foot-by-10-foot cells for twenty-two hours each day, he remains safe in his haven in the exclusive Puerto Banús resort in Marbella.

19 – BEEN THERE, DOME THAT

'No way on God's earth.'

METROPOLITAN POLICE COMMISSIONER SIR JOHN STEVENS CONCEDES THAT POLICE CORRUPTION
WILL NEVER BE ERADICATED COMPLETELY

'If only we could do this once every six months. We could do away
with the advertising department altogether.'

ANTHONY OPPENHEIMER, CHAIRMAN OF DE BEERS, ON LIFE AFTER THE DOME RAID

'You may wonder whether any large commercial organization could
have made a bigger fool of itself even if it had been trying to do so.'

NIGEL RUMFITT QC ON GROUP 4

Today, except for the Group 4 security guards, the Dome remains
empty. And as far as Group 4 is concerned, the Diamond Geezers
have had little or no effect on their work or reputation. Their
record for poor service continues unabated and unrivalled in the
security industry. Three prisoners escaped from Peterborough
Crown Court in October 2001 after tricking Group 4 security
officers and locking them in a cell. Twelve asylum seekers
absconded from the Group 4-run Oakington reception centre in
Cambridgeshire in 2002 by scaling the perimeter fence and
vanishing into the night. In 2002 Group 4 was fined £60,000 for
letting prisoners escape from Rye Hill prison.

At the start of 2002, Home Secretary David Blunkett finally gave
in to massive political pressure and announced the closure of
Campsfield House, the Group 4-run government facility which had

seen hunger strikes and rioting. On 14 January 2002 he proudly unveiled the government's £100 million flagship detention centre, Yarl's Wood in Bedfordshire, which was supposed to eliminate the bad memories associated with Campsfield. One month later, on St Valentine's Day, the thousand detainees rioted in reaction to alleged bad treatment by Group 4 staff and razed the centre to the ground. It had been built on cheap wooden frames. The building was so flimsy that when rioters had beaten the walls they visibly shook. More disturbingly, the building had not been fitted with a sprinkler system, despite advice from the fire service. Group 4 were initially investigated for the offence of corporate manslaughter. They kept such bad records that for a while it was feared that ten detainees had been burned to death in the chapel. It was not until six months after the fire, when police had sifted 140 tons of rubble and ash, that they were able to confirm that nobody had died.

In the ensuing public inquiry, the prosecutor, Nigel Rumfitt QC, branded Group 4 a 'national laughing stock' which had 'blundered' into the field of private custodial services. 'You may wonder,' he told the jury, 'whether any large commercial organization could have made a bigger fool of itself even if it had been trying to do so.' He said that the company 'fouled up' the initial stages of the police inquiry by showing photographs of suspects to potential witnesses. It organized group counselling sessions, risking the contamination of evidence, provided coaching for its officers in courtroom skills and put out a notice telling staff not to cooperate with the police. Mr Rumfitt concluded: 'All this on top of their dismal response to the original outbreak of disorder, losing control of the building within minutes.'

Despite this, Group 4 goes from strength to strength. Yarl's Wood will reopen, and Group 4 has won an £80 million contract to design, build and operate a similar 900-bed detention centre at Thurleigh in Bedford for the Immigration Service. Its largest contract to date in the UK is for the Government Communications Headquarters in Cheltenham. With a number of consortium partners, Group 4 won the £300 million contract to design and construct a new GCHQ building, roughly the size of Wembley Stadium. Group 4 will also provide facilities management for thirty years. In the meantime, Group 4 continues to rake in almost £2.2 million a year for protecting an empty Millennium Dome.

To De Beers the attempted robbery of their diamond collection from the Millennium Dome is already ancient history. De Beers' marketing wizards are currently assaulting the world's largest untapped potential diamond-buying market, China. Recent threats of competition from synthetic diamonds such as moissanite have been brushed aside by De Beers, despite the fact that thanks to vast improvements in manufacturing many jewellers find themselves unable to distinguish between them. 'But consumers don't want them,' Oppenheimer said confidently. And he's right. Moissanite lacks pedigree. If you give your girlfriend a moissanite ring (presuming you tell her, as she won't be able to tell the difference from looking) then, according to De Beers, you don't love her enough. 'Moissanite' just doesn't have the same ring as 'diamond'. There is certainly a massive potential illegal market for moissanite masquerading as diamonds, but not a market in which moissanite can compete with diamonds on a retail level, especially without the multimillion-pound advertising might of De Beers.

A rather more serious threat to De Beers may come from negative publicity. De Beers opened a new flagship store in London in 2001, after a century of occupying a behind-the-scenes role as the diamond market's monopolist. David Bowie's wife, Iman, the new face of De Beers, was used to promote the store, with a large advertising hoarding of her wearing diamonds dominating the lower half of London's Bond Street. Survival, who have long campaigned to save the indigenous populations in Africa from destruction by large companies such as De Beers, replaced the poster one night with their own version, a picture of a Bushman above the slogan: 'The Bushmen Aren't Forever.' Survival hope that such adverse publicity will eventually affect diamonds as much as it has the fur trade.

Despite this, the diamond industry in the UK was never in better shape than after the attempted Dome heist. In an interview in 2001,

Anthony Oppenheimer said: 'There's been a cultural change in the UK over the past five years. The historical view was that diamonds were for the very wealthy, for royalty and aristocracy. And now all of that is being flipped on its head. It's quite exciting.' De Beers are shrewd enough to see that we, now more than ever, are obsessed by celebrity, the new royalty, and will happily have overdrafts creaking in order to cultivate the right image. Large diamonds worn by Posh and Becks, Renée Zellweger, Guy Ritchie, J-Lo, P. Diddy and gangsta rappers have helped De Beers to create a new diamond-wearing public.

Successful criminals have long been attracted to the glitter of diamonds as ornaments of their success. They used to be used mainly to decorate their wives, girlfriends and mistresses, but over the past twenty years male gangsters across the globe have started wearing diamonds to demonstrate their power and success. If anything, the Diamond Geezers have helped to cultivate this gangster/gangsta image. Young, successful criminals don't have to try to steal their diamonds like the Diamond Geezers because they can afford to buy them and wear half a dozen or more on their fingers and wrists. Today, the diamond is a jewel for everyone, black, white, rich or not, married or single, rough and ready or soft and sophisticated. De Beers have given us all a reason to own a diamond or two.

It seems as though the Diamond Geezers may have inadvertently helped De Beers sell yet more diamonds than ever. In the opinion of Anthony Oppenheimer, the attempted theft was worth its weight in carats as far as free publicity went: 'If only we could do this once every six months. We could do away with the advertising department altogether,' he said. The millennium year was the best ever for De Beers, with sales up by almost half a *billion* dollars, from $5.24 billion in 1999 to $5.67 billion (£3.85 billion) in 2000. Things got even better in 2001 as De Beers made an incredible $744 million in profit in the first six months, up over $100 million on the same period of the previous year. By the end of 2001, the Oppenheimers decided to make a typical De Beers move and went private for more control and profit. They bought up all publicly traded shares in De Beers for £12 billion.

While De Beers got their publicity for free, the Flying Squad had to pay handsomely for theirs. The cost of having 200 officers in and around the Dome, including specialist armed officers and forensic teams as well as two helicopters, four fully crewed pursuit boats, half a dozen police cars with specialist pursuit drivers and surveillance teams pegged out along the route, on 7 November was £300,000. A similar cost was incurred on 6 November and 6 October. Four months' specialist surveillance of Tong Farm by half a dozen officers from Kent's Serious Crime Unit came to approximately £100,000 in terms of man-hours alone. Double that amount was spent on surveillance in London. The four-month trial cost £2 million, making a total of £3.5 million for Operation Magician, a Flying Squad record.

So did the Flying Squad get their money's worth? For a start, it was vital that Shatford made sure that the press got the story that the Flying Squad wanted them to get. Generally, the press and police have quite good relations in terms of promoting successful operations. Newspapers have often been used in the past to help police gather evidence. Usually, newspaper journalists would be used in sting operations, where, for example, a policeman would set up a drugs deal then call the paper, who would be present at the sting with a long lens and capture the crime in the act. On the eve of the publication of a story, the newspaper would hand over its evidence to the police, who would then arrest their suspect. Similar methods can also be useful for publicizing successes.

One newspaper was lucky enough to get a reporter and photographer in the Dome on the day of the raid, although the circumstances as to how it managed to do this are rather peculiar. On the Saturday that Cockran was recruiting Meredith in Brighton, the editor of the *Sunday People* said he received a call from an anonymous source who 'told me in what turned out to be great detail what was going to happen ... They knew it was the Dome. They told us initially it was going to be the Sunday. To be honest, my reaction was "Fuck me!" I couldn't believe it ... I rang a contact of mine, someone I know very high up in Scotland Yard. They said "Fuck me!"'

Shatford said: 'When news reached me, I was absolutely horrified. It was a major fear of mine that news of this would leak out.'

Secretly, he was probably quite pleased because a convenient deal for both parties was agreed on whereby the *Sunday People* would be given exclusive access to the Dome the moment the raid was over, and until then it would sit on the story. The *Sunday People* got its exclusive pictures, and the Flying Squad were happy because they could actually be seen by the world to be catching the criminals.

And Shatford needn't have worried about the rest of the media's and public's response. After the raid, the British press understandably accepted what they were told by Shatford, who talked about Nine Elms and Aylesford and kept saying things like, 'These were serious armed robbers,' and so on. Mad Frankie Fraser, Tony Lambrianou and Freddie Foreman gladly spoke to all the newspapers while plugging their books. It made for great copy, a story that the British public love: a bunch of cheeky gangsters tried it on and failed.

While the *Sunday People* got the pictures and the *Sun*'s headline writers rose to the occasion with 'We're Only Here for De Beers!', the *Guardian* was rather unoriginal and went for 'The Great Dome Robbery', while the *Daily Telegraph* dryly reported: 'Police Foil Smash-and-Grab Raid on Dome's £350 Million Diamonds'. Apart from a few half-hearted gripes about there being a party of schoolchildren in the Dome at the same time as the raid (they were a long way away), it was all a bit of fun to the average law-abiding newspaper reader. We admired the police's professionalism but, in Britain, we love our daring thieves, and 'Pity they got caught' was a comment often murmured during tea breaks up and down the country.

'Everybody's got a little bit of larceny in 'em,' said ex-armed robber Freddie Foreman, 'but maybe they don't have the bottle, or aren't brought up in the right environment, or because of whatever circumstances they ain't gonna do it, but they would have loved to have done the Dome and got away with it, and they wished that whoever done it had got away.'

Of course, the attempted robbery was a great coup and a fantastic opportunity to put the Flying Squad firmly in the public eye as an elite, professional unit that has put corruption scandals behind it. It was smiles and handshakes all round, as Anthony Oppenheimer said during the special thank-you ceremony at Scotland Yard at which the Met's meticulous planning and professionalism were commended for ensuring the safety of the gems. The positive effects of the coup were only to provide a temporary reprieve from the negative press, however. Speaking on 29 August 2002, Metropolitan Police Commissioner Sir John Stevens said that there was 'no way on God's earth' that the Met would ever eradicate corruption. Despite the formation of a £14 million anti-corruption 'ghost squad' in 1994, codenamed CIB3, corruption still thrives in the Flying Squad. By the end of 1998, there were 250 'rubber heels' working for CIB3 (so called because the anti-corruption officers have to move quietly), making it the biggest squad in the Met.

With the arrest of the police supergrasses McGuinness and Garner, it was a real chance for CIB3 to finally clean corruption out of the Flying Squad. 'It was a ground-breaking sting, a defining moment,' said one inspector. 'It proved to the police and the outside world we had big corruption...The whole course of policing was changed.' But it seemed as though CIB3 were unable to learn lessons from previous investigations into corrupt police, such as Operation Countryman in the 1970s, where after two thousand statements and two hundred corruption allegations, only four prosecutions were allowed and only one trial resulted in a conviction.

During CIB3's first two years of operation, seventy-four detectives were suspended, but after eight years only eight officers were convicted. Most cases either collapsed or became lost causes thanks to smart defence lawyers and the expert inside knowledge of their clients. One of the first to escape was a third man arrested with McGuinness and Garner. This senior officer confirmed that he did not know that there were drugs in the bags and thought he was helping a colleague recover office equipment when they were caught, and he was rightly acquitted. He believes that the investigation left him psychologically scarred, and he now receives his police pension early thanks to CIB3.

One success, using Garner as a witness, led to Inspector Fred May, Sergeant Eamonn Harris and PC David Howell being sentenced to seven years in 2003 for their part in stealing £200,000 from the proceeds of a £1.5 million security-van hijack in 1995. They took it from an 'inside man' at Security Express, who was hiding his share of the money in a safe house. But the strains of being a police supergrass have proved too much for Garner, who says now that, after six years of spilling the beans, he is too exhausted and psychologically traumatized to continue giving evidence against corrupt colleagues. Any further attempts to use Garner as a witness were scuppered after his solicitors said he was unfit to give evidence.

After many millions of pounds of investment and ten years in operation, CIB3 has failed to stamp out corruption. It's simply too hard to investigate people who know the system inside out and are able to frustrate their methods with ease. The Flying Squad has a long history of institutional corruption and it seems as though the foiling of a large but amateur smash-and-grab jewellery raid was just a fleeting success. While Shatford got his own personal positive publicity and a promotion, there was 'no way on earth' that the success of Operation Magician was going to help eliminate corruption and ultimately salvage the Flying Squad's reputation. Detectives work so closely with the criminal community that they can't help but become part of it.

20 – APPEALZZZ

'It would raise ... the impression that the judge had such a dim view of Betson's case that he could not be bothered to stay awake.'

EDMUND ROMILLY QC

Of course, while the Flying Squad, De Beers and Group 4 have moved on and continued with business as usual, the three surviving Diamond Geezers are currently serving their sentence as Category-A prisoners in HMP Whitemoor in Cambridgeshire. Betson had originally been sent to Long Lartin in Worcestershire but was moved to the same jail as the other two in December 2003. A Category-A prisoner is seen by the prison authorities to be one whose escape is likely to endanger the public, police and/or national security. The Diamond Geezers are under a much stricter regime than other prisoners. Category-A prisoners are the first to be locked up in their cells when there are staff shortages. Prisoners are automatically subjected to a strip-search before and after all legal and social visits. They have to be 'in vision' the whole time, and, depending on the institution, lights may be kept on at night. Their cell is subjected to regular searches, and they are moved around the jail every few weeks. Mail is screened by security staff, and telephone calls are taped. Visitors have to be cleared by police and the Home Office, a process that takes weeks.

Despite or perhaps because of this, Betson was not serving out his time idly. The Diamond Geezers' appeal had been due to take place in the summer of 2002, but thanks to Betson it took a similar course to the raid on the Dome itself, suffering continual delays and adjournments. He dismissed his original legal team shortly after Judge Coombe's sentencing and managed to persuade a very *pro-bono* human-rights solicitor, Miss Muddassar Arani, to represent him. Unfortunately, Miss Arani was not expecting to be quite so swamped by Betson, who, in spite of his dyslexia, avidly devoured the solicitor's bible, *Archbold*, and sent her letters with dozens of points on which his appeal could be based. 'I hate it when clients do that,' said Miss Arani. 'The appellant is too involved and will choose things to appeal on that will simply not work. In the end I had reduced his appeal to two points, and he wasn't happy about that at all.' Miss Arani was dismissed by Betson shortly before the appeal was due to start, and as a result it was put back to November 2003.

Betson planned to represent himself and offered his services to Ciarrocchi and Cockran, who were understandably not too keen on the idea. Ciarrocchi wanted to persuade the courts to hear his case as soon as possible, so that he could make a request to serve out the rest of his sentence in his homeland, Italy. Ciarrocchi's idea was that, once there, the Italian authorities would not be very enthusiastic about maintaining the cost of keeping him imprisoned for a crime that was not committed on Italian soil, and would perhaps release him early. This idea was vetoed by the courts at an early stage. Ciarrocchi eventually decided to appeal against his sentence rather than his conviction. Betson, as stubborn as ever, and Cockran, following in Betson's footsteps as usual, challenged their convictions and sentences. Ciarrocchi and Cockran agreed to wait until Betson was ready so that they would submit all of their appeals at the same time. Just to make things a little more difficult, Betson decided to represent himself, while Ciarrocchi and Cockran decided to stick with their original counsel, Oliver Blunt QC. Betson soon realized, however, that the task would be too huge to complete on his own, and so he decided to appeal for *pro-bono* legal assistance. But this request was refused by the Court of Appeal registrar, who argued that Betson had already wasted too much public money and time by dismissing two legal teams. Undaunted, Betson set about preparing the appeal himself and produced a remarkable forty-page document listing the issues on which he would have liked to have based his argument. When the registrar saw the document he realized that it would be better for the court if Betson did have some legal assistance. The points that Betson wanted to appeal on were so numerous and bizarre that it would take a week of the court's time to work through them all. Eventually, Edmund Romilly QC accepted the case four weeks before the appeal was due to be heard.

At 10.30 a.m. on 3 November 2003 the Diamond Geezers were summoned to the Court of Appeal at the Royal Courts of Justice in the Strand, London's legal highway. The hearing was to be held in Court 5 in the imposing Gothic building. In the public gallery of the small, dark-wood-panelled courtroom on the first floor, Detective Chief Superintendent Jon Shatford sat next to his deputy, Detective Inspector Jonathan Swinfield. In front, with their backs to the two policemen, sat Martin Heslop QC and Betson's new counsel, Edmund Romilly QC. In front of the barristers was the tall, raised bench, behind which the judges would sit. To Shatford's right, a small collection of journalists sat on the tiny reporters' bench, and opposite them was an as yet empty dock, enclosed by thick iron bars. Some friends and family of the Diamond Geezers, including the future Mrs Elisabeth Ciarrocchi, joined Shatford in the public gallery. Then the justices emerged from the back room. The assembled court rose to their feet as Lord Justice Rose, Mr Justice Poole and Mr Justice Roderick-Evans took their seats.

During the proceedings, Edmund Romilly said: 'Statements from two people present at the trial show that the judge fell asleep on a number of occasions. We have been making efforts to contact these people, so far without success.'

Lord Justice Rose asked: 'Has the judge not admitted that he did fall asleep?'

Mr Romilly said he was not sure whether the judge had admitted falling asleep once or more than once. 'Statements I have seen suggest that the learned judge fell asleep not just during a closing speech but also during the evidence,' he said.

Lord Justice Rose replied: 'If that happened, it would be necessary to show that, in consequence, part of the evidence did not find its way into the judge's summing-up, or something of that sort.'

Remarkably, Judge Coombe did confess that he had fallen asleep during the trial, but he maintains to this day that it was only on one occasion, during Oliver Blunt's closing speech, and that it could not possibly have affected the fairness of the trial or his judgement.

The appeal judges also made it clear that they were not amused by Betson's unique approach to the appeals process: 'This appellant [Betson] dispensed with his original counsel,' said Lord Justice Rose, 'and in due course other leading counsel were assigned to him at public expense. He has since dispensed with their services as well. He then drafted a forty-page document on his own grounds of appeal. By this stage the case was to be heard on 19 May 2003, but his new counsel requested more time to consider the information that Mr Betson wanted to put forward. The appeal hearing was rescheduled for 26 July with a time estimate of one day to hear his case. Then his new counsel changed that estimate on 10 July to three days. The earliest, then, that the court could afford this time was today, 3 November. On 4 September the court was informed that both solicitors and counsel had withdrawn from the case. They did not manage to lodge any new grounds of appeal. The appellant's third application for legal assistance was refused by the registrar but, after the appellant submitted this forty-page document, Mr Romilly came into the case. Now Mr Romilly submits that he needs more time. We have taken the trouble to list the history of this case because we would like to make it abundantly clear that this will be the last time that this case will be delayed. It will be heard on whatever new date will be fixed.'

The Diamond Geezers never actually made an appearance in court that day. Like the raid itself, the appeal was temporarily aborted, adjourned for seven weeks to give Mr Romilly sufficient time to prepare. But what was it that Betson was so keen for the Diamond Geezers' appeal to be about? Well, he wanted to bring up at least twelve issues, from the adverse effects of pre-trial publicity to whether the real diamonds were ever in the Dome, but none of what he wanted to say was going to do him any good, according to his various legal teams, and would in fact only land him in hot water with the appeal judges, who would think that he was wasting valuable court time. Despite Betson's protests, Romilly savagely whittled down his list so that just two of his original points remained, along with a couple of new ones, the most promising of which were that the judge fell asleep and therefore they might not have had a fair trial, and that the Diamond Geezers were not armed and so were entitled to a reduction in their sentence.

This time, on Wednesday 22 January 2004 at 10.30 a.m., nothing was going to stop the Appeal Court judges from having their final say. But things didn't start at all smoothly, as Ciarrocchi claimed that he wanted to join his two friends in appealing against his conviction as well as sentence. Mr Romilly professed to Lord Justice Rose that this was the first that he had heard of this. Betson and Cockran refused to appear in the dock until it was sorted out. Eventually, using the logic that if Betson and Cockran were successful then it would naturally follow that Ciarrocchi could appeal on the same grounds, just Betson and Cockran entered and confirmed their names before sitting, surrounded by four prison officers. Betson, wearing a dark blue shirt, was clean-shaven and impassive. Cockran, wearing a pale blue shirt, sat with his arms folded and rubbed his eyes, which had bags under them. They both smiled at friends and relatives in the packed public gallery.

The main ground of appeal against conviction related to the already mentioned allegation that Judge Coombe fell asleep during the trial. There are several precedents in British law that relate to judges falling asleep. The first occurred back in 1961 when the trial judge dozed off during a court-martial hearing. Ernest Edworthy, a Royal Army Pay Corps officer, had been court-martialled for fraudulent financial dealings while serving in Sierra Leone. Edworthy appealed, and the summing-up of the learned judge (Mr Acland-Hood) was studied. It was discovered that the judge must have been asleep because in his summing-up he failed to refer to crucial information that was presented during the trial. Edworthy was acquitted.

Ten years later, in 1971, at the Old Bailey, two brothers, Alan and Keith Langham, had been found guilty of a particularly gruesome murder in which Charles Levett, an elderly Hastings shopkeeper, had been stabbed fourteen times, twice in the back and twelve times in the chest, during a burglary gone wrong. Levett had been stabbed so hard that two knives had broken off inside his body during the attack. The two men were found guilty and sentenced to life by Judge Crichton, but they told their solicitor that they were convinced that the judge had fallen asleep more than once during the proceedings. The solicitor agreed: 'When the evidence was coming to an end,' he said, 'and counsel's speeches were beginning, the judge at twelve noon was sitting with his head resting on his hands, his eyes shut and his head nodding, and for approximately the next fifteen minutes he was manifestly asleep.' They were given grounds to appeal on this point. If they were successful, then it would have been embarrassing for British justice. These two obviously guilty men would have been found not to have had a fair trial and would have had to be released. The three judges, including Lord Widgery, the then Lord Chief Justice, put their heads together and came back to the court with an answer. They concluded that His Honour Judge Crichton had simply been 'thinking with his eyes shut'. The appeal was not granted.

But in the Diamond Geezers' case, the trial judge had admitted that he had fallen asleep. The two witness statements were produced and read out by Mr Romilly. The statements, however, were inadmissible because they were just that, i.e. not affidavits. They contained a lot of supposition and personal opinion. In addition, the clerk had still not been found. But the *Panorama* researcher had been tracked down and was in court. The judges could not dismiss this claim so easily. The Diamond Geezers were clearly guilty of attempting an audacious crime. It would be extremely embarrassing for the judicial system and the police to free three men after they had been convicted following a massive police operation and trial that had cost the British taxpayer £3.5 million. Even a costly retrial would be too much for the courts to bear.

The judges, Lord Justice Rose, Mr Justice Poole and Mr Justice Roderick-Evans, listened attentively as Mr Romilly, in a considered and softly spoken manner, put forward the first argument for his clients, followed by a slightly louder Oliver Blunt. Mr Romilly argued that the judge had nodded off on numerous occasions, but that doing so only during closing speeches would still have been prejudicial: 'It would raise ... the impression that the judge had such a dim view of Betson's case that he could not be bothered to stay awake. The fact that witnesses say that he was snoring adds another feature, in that it makes the conduct more blatant. Anyone can be forgiven for momentary lapses of concentration, but it is another matter if there is sleepfulness accompanied by noises associated with sleep, drawing attention to the person who is asleep and deflecting the jury's attention.'

The defence also attacked Judge Coombe for acting more like an advocate than a judge and for doing most of the prosecution's work for them. Comparing the trial to a cricket match, Oliver Blunt said that at times 'the judge really abandoned the umpirical role, took a few paces back for his run-up to bowl and, bounding in off a long run, seemed to pepper Mr Betson with a series of bouncers'.

The arguments all heard, Lord Justice Rose adjourned the court and the three judges retired to consider their decision. Fifteen minutes later they were ready. Journalists scrambled for a seat as word spread through the corridors outside that they had already reached a decision. They then sat, looking like darts players, with their eyes narrowed in concentration and their pens poised above their notebooks. Shatford was sitting straight-backed on one of the uncomfortable benches in the public gallery, anxious that his investigation should not fall apart due to a sleepy judge. The families of the Diamond Geezers held each other's hands. The two appellants entered and stood, no doubt their legs weak from nerves and anticipation. Their Honours entered from the judges' door and the court rose silently.

Lord Justice Rose said: 'We have considered the appeal and have reached a decision. Raymond John Betson and William Thomas Cockran, you claim that you did not receive a fair trial because the judge fell asleep. We disagree and refuse to grant you leave to appeal against your conviction. We will explain our decision tomorrow after we have heard the arguments for the appeal against sentence in this court tomorrow at 10.30 a.m.'

As journalists dashed off to file their stories, Shatford breathed a small sigh of relief. Betson and Cockran did not betray any emotion as the decision was announced, but as they were led away they did manage small smiles for their friends and families in the public gallery.

'Better luck for today,' one BBC journalist whispered to Betson's solicitor the following Thursday morning.

'Well, it could hardly have gone much worse yesterday,' he replied. The feeling among the legal team was that while their arguments were sound, they weren't going to cut much slack with the three judges, especially Lord Justice Rose, who is not one to be easily swayed, 'particularly on delicate points of law such as this involves', said one of Betson's legal counsel.

The first part of the appeal against their sentence was the most likely to buy them some time. As Shatford said: 'I suspect that they will get a couple of years off because they will be able to say, "We weren't carrying guns."' Now that the event had faded somewhat from public memory, the defence hoped that it would be acceptable for the court to recognize this and reduce the sentence slightly. The defence's hopes also rested on the Sentencing Advisory Panel's recommendations. Lord Justice Rose did concede that 'the argument that there was an absence of firearms was a powerful one'. He listened to the arguments of Mr Blunt regarding the Sentencing Advisory Panel and said: 'Yes, but these conclusions are simply the result of a consultation and may not ever be applied in law.' The defence team then threw everything they had at the judge, with Mr Romilly sounding rather desperate when he said that all the Diamond Geezers would have escaped with were the fakes that had been placed there 'the day before' and that this should mitigate their sentence. But only two arguments counted. They were not carrying guns and, while the raid was meticulously planned and exceptionally audacious, it was planned in such a way as to cause no harm to any member of the public.

As the judges retired to make their decision, they made the startling announcement that they would take only about fifteen minutes.

On their return, Lord Justice Rose said: 'It is perfectly plain that judges should remain awake, but Judge Coombe's summing-up had been carefully prepared, comprehensive, accurate as to the law and detailed as to the evidence.' The three judges concluded that while the judge may have nodded off, no one brought it to the court's attention at the time – perhaps allowing the defendants 'two bites of the cherry' because if the verdict didn't go their way then they would have a sound basis of appeal. Lord Justice Rose also said that while the trial lasted for three months, the judge could only have been asleep for a tiny fraction of the time. 'The judge was clearly alert for most of the trial,' he said.

Turning to the question of sentencing, Lord Justice Rose said that the Dome raid had been 'meticulously planned' and 'the rewards if successful were not just large, but immense, to an extent never previously contemplated in this country, amounting as they did to more than £200 million'.

Then they listed the witnesses who had said that the JCB entering the Dome looked like a tank, and included the testimony of Jason Forrest, the chef, and the police officers who were in fear of their lives. On mentioning Mr Monroe's statement that 'if anyone had been behind that door, then they wouldn't have stood a chance', Cockran rolled his eyes skywards and muttered something to Betson. The three men's brows became more and more furrowed as it seemed the judges were not going to offer them any sort of reduction at all. Betson started to bite his nails. Ciarrocchi, a mere stick of a boy next to the bulk of Betson and Cockran, leaned forward and held his hands together against his mouth, his index fingers steepled so that they touched the tip of his nose. Cockran sat with his arms folded, and one hand moved up to cover his mouth as if he was trying to restrain himself from a verbal outburst.

But then Lord Justice Rose said: 'We think it important, even though this is, as we have described it, an abnormal case, to pay particular regard to the fact that firearms were not carried, still less used.' They ruled that the sentences originally imposed were 'excessive'.

'In light of this,' he continued, 'we have decided that Raymond John Betson and William Thomas Cockran's sentence will be reduced from eighteen years to fifteen years and that Aldo Ciarrocchi's sentence will be reduced from fifteen years to twelve years.' Finally, the Diamond Geezers had got a break, albeit a small one. The three men smiled at their supporters as they were led away.

AFTERWORD

'At least we had the balls to try.'

WOULD-BE DOME ROBBER, WILLIAM COCKRAN

'He who dares wins, Rodney.'

DEL BOY TO RODNEY TROTTER, *ONLY FOOLS AND HORSES*

Today the Dome remains empty. A few Londoners seeking a bit of peace and quiet sit on one of the many benches that surround the structure and read the paper or a good novel. Some seagulls whirr overhead. North Greenwich tube station does not have a rush hour. Time stands still at the Dome. Although the structure appears to be perfectly brand new, it does have one blemish. If you approach the Dome from the north-west and pass through Gate 10, you'll see a few scratches and marks on the inner side of the structure. This is the Dome's only scar from the day when six men with two vans, a boat and a JCB tried to get away with the impossible crime.

When Shatford is asked why, after big robberies such as Brinks Mat and the Great Train Robbery, with the lengthy deterrent sentences they attract and all the trouble that comes with them, the Diamond Geezers decided that it was worth trying to steal the most precious diamond collection in the world for comparatively little reward, he said: 'Clearly, they honestly believed and were very, very confident that they were going to get away with it. They were confident with the people they were working with. They looked at the job and clearly thought that it was feasible. I mean, they never, ever expected us to be there; their total surprise was quite something.'

The main reason why the Diamond Geezers were so confident was largely thanks to De Beers and Group 4, who provided them with such a vulnerable target. Although Anthony Oppenheimer said, 'Of course, we are extremely grateful that the real diamonds were kept safe,' and token donations have been made to Victim Support and the Met Voluntary Fund, De Beers were getting the best advertising for a bargain-basement price and were under no obligation to contribute to the massive cost of Operation Magician which, of course, was paid for by the public.

I asked De Beers one last time how much they had sold the Millennium Star to De Beers LV, their retail chain, for: 'That is a private matter between the two parties. You can try to ask De Beers LV if you like [I did, and, no, they didn't tell me]. What I can say is that it is useless to guess because buying a rare diamond is like buying a rare piece of art – it is worth what it is worth to the person who values it highly enough to buy it.'

For the Diamond Geezers, the diamonds were worth a lot of trouble, but cost them a lifetime (their combined sentences, even taking into account the appeal, came to sixty-five years). But as armed robbers go, they were pretty small fry. Armed robbers fall into three broad categories: amateur, intermediate and professional. Amateur robbers form the largest group by far and are categorized by their haphazard, opportunistic approach, often with little awareness of the lengthy prison sentences they could (and usually do) end up serving. They tend to operate alone, aim for relatively small amounts of money and are motivated by desperation: for example, to pay off debts to drug pushers. Amateurs often carry out their crimes under the influence of alcohol and drugs, with no idea of how much money to expect. Many later express deep embarrassment at their incompetence and are reluctant to reveal exactly how much money they had stolen because the amounts were so pitifully small.

Their stories range from the tragic to the comic. Martin, currently serving five years in Wormwood Scrubs for armed robbery, explained: 'Basically, it was the last straw. I was on the settee at 12 o'clock at night and my daughter was being sick in the next room. I said to the missus, "Can you smell it?" She said, "Yeah," and I ran into my little daughter's room and gave her to the missus. She had sick over her. Then the electric went, and I didn't have a penny. You know what I mean, not one penny. Couldn't put the electric on. So I stood there with two candles while she was looking after the kid, trying to clean up the vomit, and that's when I decided enough is enough. I thought, yeah, I'll do it.' After he was caught and jailed, Martin was so ashamed of committing the crime that he never allowed his daughter to visit him in prison.

An extreme example of amateurish ineptness is the case of the eighteen-year-old who, fed up with the drudgery of working in a dead-end factory job, decided to rob a security van with a kitchen knife. The guards obeyed the young man's threats but handed over a decoy cash box full of shredded paper. Thinking that he'd succeeded, the young robber fled around the corner and changed his clothes to avoid detection. He was spotted by a passer-by, who told the police what he'd seen. When the police examined the clothes, they discovered his name sewn neatly into the collar of his shirt, which also formed part of his work uniform.

It is clear that the Diamond Geezers were not *this* inept. They had made and followed a detailed plan and already had between them a long history of involvement in petty crime. 'They tried to carry out a major robbery,' said Professor Roger Matthews, criminologist and author of *Armed Robbery*. 'It was audacious, and although one might categorize them as "intermediates" they obviously had aspirations to be professionals. But like a large percentage of people who carry out robberies, they were fairly incompetent.'

Indeed, when you analyse the modus operandi of the gang, it does seem that it was a miracle that they made it as far as they did. Inexperienced robbers will tend to choose targets reasonably close to home, more professional robbers will normally be prepared to travel further afield, and among more professional robbers it is not unusual for more than one escape route to be mapped out prior to the robbery. For the persistent armed robber, violence has to become part of one's persona. In order to commit oneself to robbery, one must readily display a commitment to violent behaviour. The Diamond Geezers went out of their way to avoid being seen as violent.

Among intermediate groups, the takings from robberies are typically used to finance both legitimate and illegitimate business activities as well as to deal in drugs or other commodities. Betson needed the money because his 'duty-free importation business' had gone pear-shaped and he wanted to escape the climes of South-East London for the sandy shores of Marbella. In fact, the more one looks at Betson, Cockran, Ciarrocchi and Adams, the more obvious it is that they were rank amateurs. In particular, Ciarrocchi's youthful penchant for joke-shop materials and his short criminal record are the hallmarks of a first-timer. Similarly, Adams was a late starter as a criminal, and for reasons that will only ever really have been known to himself (although it can, of course, be speculated that he was looking to escape the drudgery of his lonely existence) decided to join the Diamond Geezers at the last minute. Apart from Millman, a relatively unsuccessful professional long-term lag, Betson and Cockran were most definitely aspiring towards the intermediate category. In fact they might be categorized as 'intermediate diversifiers'. This group has a reasonable level of planning, long histories of relatively petty criminal involvement – for example, handling stolen goods, car theft, small frauds and duty evasion – and are inclined to take part in large heists if the circumstances are right. In a number of cases these diversifiers are invited to participate in a major theft or robbery planned by others, something that we have seen to have been the case with the Diamond Geezers.

Despite this, Shatford said that criminals 'walk in fear' of Betson and Cockran. As well as Aylesford and Nine Elms, he referred to a job in Barking, Essex, where in 1996 £3 million was robbed from a security van on an industrial estate in 1996. Shatford said they knew then that Betson was responsible and that he and Cockran were 'financing other violent armed robberies', from which they netted a total of £15 million. But Shatford was never able to link Betson and

Cockran to any of these raids. As Judge Coombe said at the trial: 'There is no evidence, any whatsoever, to link them to these crimes, none whatsoever.' Both the Nine Elms and Aylesford attempted robberies were very professionally executed, violent and relied on instilling fear into the security guards in the vans. This does not sit well with the modus operandi of the Diamond Geezers.

From looking at the backgrounds of the Diamond Geezers, it is evident that they were not quite as professional as the police portrayed them. But at the time of their arrest and trial, the police spin had helped to seal their fate. Who on earth would believe that a bunch of amateurs would make a very public attempt at what would have been the theft of the millennium? It appears that the Diamond Geezers were probably the most unfortunate criminal collective in the world. Prior to the raid itself, there was the Diamond Geezers' own plain bad luck, bad timing and amateurishness. The notice saying that the real diamonds were not at the vault was never displayed and Betson even visited the Dome when the stones were in Antwerp. The gang failed to spot that they were being watched over a five-month period by hundreds of police. The shutter at the entry point into the Dome, which had been up each time Betson had visited, was down on the day, so they had to charge through it. The steel casing that covered the glass in the diamond vault was not used any more; if it was, then the job would have been a non-starter. The police were flooding the Dome with dozens of detectives, but nothing leaked out.

Shatford is wrong to say that Britain is a safer place now that the Diamond Geezers are locked away. Britain would be safer if the mastermind, Jack Carter, had been imprisoned. Instead, Carter is already back on the capital's streets – the Diamond Geezers, meanwhile, still have many years to reflect on what life might have been like had they not been tempted into taking a shot at the crime of the millennium. Operation Magician simply caught the little fish and, in the words of Mad Frankie Fraser: 'Operation Magician, like all magical tricks, was an illusion.'

Looking at Betson, Ciarrocchi and Cockran, one can't help but be reminded of the hapless Del Boy, Rodney and Grandpa of *Only Fools and Horses* fame. They should have known better, but as Great Train Robber Ronnie Biggs said to Diamond Geezer Bill Cockran when he found out what he was in for: 'Bloody 'ell. We never learn, do we?'

SELECT BIBLIOGRAPHY

An excellent overview of modern-day corruption in the Flying Squad and police force in general is given in *Bent Coppers: The Inside Story of Scotland Yard's Battle Against Corruption* by Graeme McLagan (Weidenfeld and Nicolson, 2003). For a more historical perspective see *Bent Coppers: A Survey of Police Corruption* by James Morton (Little, Brown, 1993). Ex-undercover policeman Duncan McLaughlin gives an admirable no-nonsense account of police life in *The Filth: The Explosive Inside Story of Scotland Yard's Top Undercover Cop* (Mainstream Publishing, 2002).

For the definitive account of how De Beers took control of the diamond markets see *The Diamond Invention* by Edward Jay Epstein (Hutchinson, 1982). The most detailed description of the modern-day diamond industry is given by Janine Roberts in *Glitter and Greed: The Secret World of the Diamond Cartel* (Disinformation Company, 2004).

British crime families are well-documented in James Morton's comprehensive tome *Gangland Today* (Time Warner, 2003) which features a section on the Adamses, as does Wensley Clarkson's *Gangsters* (John Blake, 2003). For a fascinating look at robbery from an academic's perspective see *Armed Robbery* by Professor Roger Matthews (Willan Publishing, 2002).

The criminal activities of Semyon Mogilevich and the Russian Mafia are covered in detail in award-winning investigative journalist Robert I. Friedman's absorbing book, *Red Mafiya* (Little, Brown, 2000). Gordon Thomas and Martin Dillon also deal with the Russian Mafia's influence in Europe in *The Assassination of Robert Maxwell, Israel's Superspy* (Robson Books, 2002).

INDEX